THE FUTURE
IN THE STARS

THE FUTURE IN THE STARS

THE ASTROLOGICAL MESSAGE FOR 2012 AND BEYOND

Alison Chester-Lambert

FINDHORN PRESS

© Alison Chester-Lambert 2010

The right of Alison Chester-Lambert to be identified as the author of this
work has been asserted by him in accordance with the Copyright, Designs
and Patents Act 1998.

Published in 2010 by Findhorn Press, Scotland

ISBN 978-1-84409-505-6

A CIP record for this title is available from the British Library.

Edited and typeset by Maggie Aldred
Front cover design by Richard Crookes
Illustrations by Robbi Lambert
Printed in the European Union

1 2 3 4 5 6 7 8 9 17 16 15 14 13 12 11 10

Published by
Findhorn Press
117-121 High Street,
Forres IV36 1AB,
Scotland, UK

t +44 1309 690 582
f +44 131 777 2711
e info@findhornpress.com

www.findhornpress.com

I dedicate this book to *you*! A divine child
who, by your awareness of these gods
and goddesses, will help to raise their love
and support in the spiritual consciousness of
the human race. For when we learn of
our planetary energies, we connect with the
soul of the Universe.

CONTENTS

Changes are Happening

"We shall not cease from exploration.
And the end of all our exploring
Will be to arrive where we started.
And know the place for the first time."

T. S. Elliot

Lo! There is a star in the east...

Two thousand years ago three astrologers rode into Jerusalem on camels and announced that a new star in the east heralded the birth of a Messiah. This remains one of the most famous translation jobs done by astrologers and hopefully, this book follows in that tradition!

The story this time revolves around the discovery of new planets in our Solar System and the re-classifying of others. These changes herald a transformation of 2,000 years of spiritual understanding and patriarchal domination. History is being written and something very special is happening.

Okay, so what's a solar system?

It's the name we give to planets and objects revolving around a sun. Each star in the sky is a sun so, as you can imagine, there are numerous solar systems! When we speak of *the* Solar System, we mean ours. In the last 2,000 years, knowledge of our Solar System has had two periods of considerable change. The first was from 1610 to 1846, and the second one is now. The first one coincided with the arrival of the scientific, industrial and cultural revolution.

The one we are in now started in 1930, followed by an explosion of discoveries from 2004 to 2006.

This book takes six of the recent planetary discoveries and changes to the Solar System and explains what these mean to the human race as a whole and to the individual. Meaning is drawn from the myths surrounding the name of a planet, the events surrounding its discovery and an in-depth knowledge of astrology, but without the jargon!

How can changes to the Solar System convey new spiritual meaning?

Strange as it may sound, important finds in astronomy always coincide with major shifts in the evolution of the human race and spiritual understanding.

The last really big change in our understanding of our Solar System began in the 17th century, when Galileo devised an astronomical telescope and was imprisoned for finding the Moons of Jupiter and daring to state that the Earth *wasn't* the centre of the Universe... *and* it revolved around the Sun.[1] He also discovered Neptune at this time, but was so excited by Jupiter's Moons that he did not even register Neptune as a planet.[2] Fundamental discoveries were being made in our Solar System at this time, such as discovering why the Moon hadn't fallen to Earth. Mathematical calculations were also leading to the discoveries of more planets. Galileo, both a scientist and astrologer, published a book about his discoveries entitled *The Starry Messenger.*

The centre of the civilised world shifted to Northern Europe from Italy and the dogmatic Catholic Church. Isaac Newton and the new Republic of England emerged from the grip of the Middle Ages and a scientific revolution began.[3] As Uranus and Neptune were discovered, revolutions of all kinds were in full swing.

So, what's happening these days? Read any holistic or spiritual

magazine published in the early years of the 21st century and you are
told of "Changes to Earth Consciousness" and "Ascendance to Higher
Dimensions". People who listen to angels and go to reiki classes were
whispering of awakenings. From Leighton Buzzard to Newcastle-
under-Lyme, something was stirring.

From 2003 a great many things were happening in the world of science
and quantum physics. Phenomenal discoveries were emerging. But
the jargon was hard to understand and explain, so the journalists and
public gave a yawn and turned to the sports page!

Changes are certainly happening with regard to the Earth's climate
and even the planet itself is changing. The magnetic pole is galloping
to a different North.[4] Fortunately, global navigation satellite systems
mean we don't have to rely on magnetic compasses any more.

It seems that when we make breakthroughs in knowledge in *any* sphere
of life, other areas grow and change, even if they seem unrelated.

In astrology, the recent changes to our known Solar System will hold
strong signposts and clues about the years to come, since these energies
will become a feature of our lives as they walk side by side with us.
The meanings, myths and circumstances surrounding the discovery
and naming of these new planets or objects will forever be what this
planet symbolises, both personally and in the Collective. The name is
particularly important, as they are always named after deities (gods and
goddesses) from mythology. This means we have all those mythological
stories to tell us of that planet's meaning.

That fact is probably the most unbelievable in astrology because it is
astro*nomers* and not astrologers that name planets. An astronomer is
a scientist who measures the heavens using complicated mathematical
formulae and associated complex instruments. He does *not* believe
that they convey meaning. An astro*loger* is spiritually motivated and
associates behaviour and meaning with a planet. They believe that
the planets affect the Earth, the human race and every single human
being. The planets symbolise energies that influence us.

So how come an astro*nomer*, sitting on a deserted mountaintop with a telescope, happens to pick the right name? The answer is mysterious and magical, since the scientist astronomer is under the influence of the planet and the planet, therefore, 'tells' the discoverer what to call it. He would have been studying it at length, immersed in its energy and meaning. Mike Brown, the astronomer in charge of the team that discovered most of the dwarf planets which form the basis of this book, said of one of them, Eris, that she behaved so like her mythological character, it almost made him believe in astrology.[5]

Another influence on the astronomer is the current Collective issues, fashion and general feelings at the 'eureka' moment. As cut off as the astronomer might be, he is still connected to these influences spiritually, through the ether. When he names a planet he acts as spokesperson, becoming the mouthpiece for a cosmic web of connected energy.

How our knowledge of the Solar System has changed

If we go back thousands of years BC, it is more than likely that the great civilisations knew much more than we do now about astrology and our Solar System. For some reason the coming of a one god religion brought about a *de*-volution of this knowledge. The contents of ancient libraries were burnt, and many great secrets of the Universe were lost forever. We have a few scraps and hints, but we haven't regained enough intellectual, technological and spiritual ground to understand what these mean, although recently there does seem to be some progress. The trouble is, we are mainly in the hands of archaeologists, who find it difficult to look up and be inspired by the stars. (Sorry guys!)

The model of the Solar System from around year 01 AD to about 1610 AD didn't change much. It consisted of all the planets we can see with the naked eye, with the Earth in the middle (*diagram 1*).

This image of our Solar System, with the 'flat' Earth at the centre of the Universe, demonstrated how intellectually and spiritually restricted the human race was. Cultural growth was relatively limited, and our

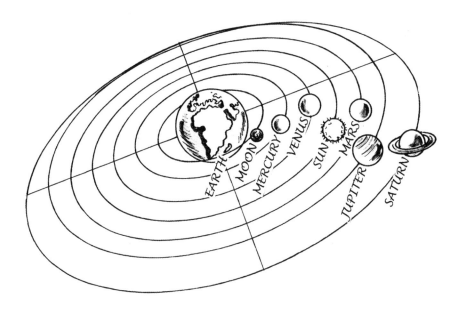

1 *How the Solar System was thought to look until 17th Century*

knowledge of the Solar System reflected this. Saturn was the extent of the planets that were known, (the outermost planet that can be seen with the naked eye) and it represented the limit placed on growth and evolution.

In astrology, the innermost planets represent those parts of our personality that we most recognise and control. Our overall ego and emotional vulnerability, how we communicate, what we desire and value, and the energy we use to obtain all that. The outermost planets, Jupiter and Saturn, represent growth and restriction. That was all we needed to know. Ourselves, and what restricted us.

It is interesting to note that this patriarchal time had two feminine planets and five masculine ones, reflecting the bias towards the masculine.

The Solar System after 1849 has the Sun at its centre. Two planets have been added to the outer edge, and an asteroid belt of smaller objects is now known to exist between Mars and Jupiter (*diagram 2*).

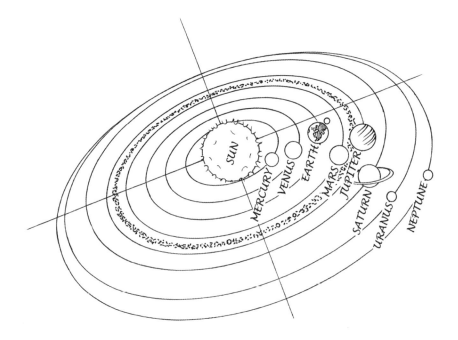

2 *The Solar System after 1849*

Okay, so at least we now have things in the right order. The discovery of Uranus and Neptune symbolised the beginning of a cosmic or bigger world view. Universal energies were coming into play and we would start to see the human race as part of a much bigger plan.

The asteroids were generally ignored until the recent big change. There was a flurry of scientific data when they were discovered around 1800, then they sunk into obscurity. Strangely, the four largest asteroids were all named after goddesses, representing feminine energy. Perhaps it wasn't the right time because the world wasn't ready to pay homage to matriarchal influence again. Now, one of the asteroids is part of the new changes and this recognition has coincided with the re-emergence of the feminine or goddess universal energies once more.

Diagram 3 shows the addition of Pluto-Charon, Eris, Makemake, Haumea and Sedna in the outer reaches of the Solar System, and the recently acknowledged and promoted dwarf planet Ceres that was

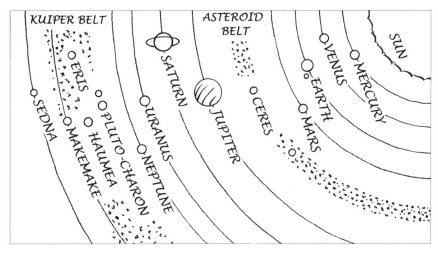

3 *The latest re-organisation of the Solar System for the 21st century*

already within the asteroid belt of the old Solar System, but had been ignored. This organisation was formally announced in August 2006.

The discovery of a whole new region of the Solar System

The discoveries in the outer reaches of the Solar System were partly made possible because of more sophisticated instruments, but also because the astronomers started looking in a different part of the sky. All the known planets in earlier times were spinning around the Sun in a straight line, or on a flat plane, like looking at a plate from side on. So they made the assumption that any other planets farther out would be the same. Pluto, discovered in 1930, was the odd one out. It wasn't in a line with the others, but at an angle. So Pluto was the first messenger to tell us there was more. He seemed to say, "Don't follow the same old line of thinking, step outside of your safe, known boundaries". So the astronomers started to look elsewhere... and they found much more! A remote doughnut-shaped ring around the Solar System that was named the Kuiper Belt and comprises of many objects and rocks, some as large as planets. They symbolised a whole new world of discovery in the fields of science and technology, plus the expected spiritual growth and future experiences of the human race or Collective.

The new planets discovered in the outer reaches of our Solar System caused problems with the definition of the term 'planet'. Were all the new objects to be called 'planets'? If so, they would have to keep re-writing the textbooks every time a new one was discovered. In August 2006, the International Astronomical Union (IAU) got together and decided on a definition that meant anything new would not be called a planet; it would be a 'dwarf planet' instead. The only problem was, this new definition would have to apply to Pluto. He could no longer be called a planet and so was demoted to 'dwarf planet' status. There was press and public outcry, and letters were written to the *Times*. Arguments abounded in the usually stuffy world of astronomy as the scientists argued about who had discovered what, and what it should be called. It was decided to name one of the new planets after the Greek goddess of strife and rivalry, so that was pretty apt!

The new discoveries were given the names of gods and goddesses from ancient world civilisations as far apart as Iceland, Greece and Polynesia. The mythology surrounding each of them tells us about the things that will become important to the human race in the 21st century. Sedna speaks of weather, flooding, huge global movements of water and the plight of sea creatures. Pluto-Charon symbolise nuclear energy and scientific breakthroughs in sub-atomic physics that will reveal other, invisible dimensions. These other dimensions of science will prove to include the mythical Underworld of our ancient spiritual texts. Makemake represents fertility, human creation and its issues, such as indigenous populations, pandemics and over population. With Haumea, another Polynesian deity, we get a clearer understanding of how deity and spirit resides in all matter and material things, leading to changes in religion and spiritual beliefs. Haumea also represents new spiritual understanding of Mother Nature's cycles and the feminine energy which is the ultimate power behind creation. Ceres will also alter our attitude to death and the soul's passage into other dimensions. Another of her issues will be world food shortages. This leaves Eris, who represents the choice between strife and rivalry or ethics, natural justice and determined endeavour.

We will discover what our world was created from, why and how

Put very simply, earth, matter, and order is created from fire, spirit and chaos. Energy takes on form and becomes matter. This is called the Big Bang in science, or the 'Fall' in orthodox religion.[6] Our world was created out of another, a formless soup of divine potential – the deities. We will come to understand more of the mighty, invisible forces controlling this delicate balance. The new planets speak of our ability to find answers to these deeply hidden, invisible forces and our understanding of the spiritual energies that underpin our world will expand as rapidly as our science. The scientists call it 'dark' matter and 'dark' energy. Dark simply means invisible, or in another dimension, something completely undetectable. We will discover, amongst other things, the 'Underworld'. The stories of burning hell fires and purgatory of the Catholic Church were actually based on their worst earthly experiences, which were the volcanoes of Italy. Two of the world's major tectonic plates meet in Italy, giving the country its reputation as the most earthquake and volcano-prone in Europe. This became a feature of their religion, since civilisations will always use the images around them to understand the spiritual. It is time to change that image, since we now have a much bigger Cosmos to look at and not just a region of Earth.

We will also be pushed into greater responsibility for physical Earth in terms of raw materials, food, crops and nature. Mother Nature and the primordial feminine, or matriarch, is re-emerging.

Well that's a quick overview of their meaning, but now it's time to see what each of these separate new energies is about in detail.

2

Cool Science

*"The entire Universe is this gigantic loaf with
many other slices, potentially. So our Universe
could be one slice, and a different parallel
Universe could be living on a different slice."*

Brian Greene, physicist

Before we look at what some of the new planets are symbolising, it would be helpful to try to understand the new realms that science is discovering. As we saw in the first chapter, the two things are linked and some of the new planets are describing these new realms. I have tried to make this chapter really simple, but in truth the new scientific discoveries are astounding. If you do find it difficult to take it in all at once, just go to the back of this chapter where I have written an explanation simple enough for my mother to understand. That should be enough for you to comprehend the rest of the book.

Why are we making all these discoveries now?

Science now has very powerful instruments that can see things one millionth the size of a speck of dust and it is revealing things stranger than even science fiction could imagine. It is called quantum physics or particle physics, since the tiniest bits of all are called 'particles'.

Likewise, there have been big improvements in space telescopes. Some have been launched into orbit around the Earth and these can see the stars much more clearly than before. This has led to leaps in our understanding of the Universe, although each discovery gives us more questions than answers. One of the most wondrous things to behold is how science, spiritual beliefs and mythology are all converging. However, it has to be said that it is scientific understanding that is changing the most, and revealing realities that make complete sense of ancient spiritual texts written thousands of years ago. The academic community previously discounted these texts as gibberish. Scientists and spiritual intellectuals will deny this converging of opinion, since neither is keen to be associated with an enemy previously thought to be un-enlightened. However, the similarities between them just grow every day. This will become obvious as you read on.

What is matter? What is our Universe made of?

Everything that you see around you, the chairs and furniture in the room, this book, your body and even the water vapour that you exhale, can all be broken down into smaller and smaller pieces. The chair is made of wood, wood is made of cells, cells have molecules, and the molecules are made of atoms. And up until the 20th century that was the extent of our knowledge. It was thought that the atoms were the hard bits that gave matter its rigidity. And when microscopes were invented that could measure the *really* tiny, the scientists assumed that they were on the verge of looking inside the solid bit.

But they looked right through the atom and still they couldn't find much that was solid! Atoms are almost empty caverns. There is a bit at the centre called a nucleus, *but*, the nucleus in the atom has the same proportions as a fly in a cathedral![1] That's a lot of empty space. The nucleus is made up of 'particles', hence the name 'particle physics'.

Whirling around the nucleus are 'electrons,' but these aren't solid either. They are described as "weird excitations and vibrations of invisible field energy."[2]

Put simply, it is like the spokes of a bicycle wheel that appear solid when the wheel is spinning fast. They would feel quite solid if you were to stroke them with a feather, but when the wheel stops the spokes don't add up to much at all, and the feather could easily pass through.

The spinning bits of energy have organised themselves into a 'lattice' that holds together and repels things or feels resistant to the touch. So when your finger touches your arm, both feel solid. This illusion of solidness is in all matter and every material thing in the Universe including you and me. A biologist says "Physical atoms are made up of vortices of energy that spin and vibrate." They then "had to come to realise that the Universe is not made of matter suspended in empty space but energy."[3] As energy is the same thing as 'spirit', this confirms we are spiritual beings.

A parallel Universe or other dimension that supports ours

But it's even stranger than that. Occasionally particles just appear and then disappear. They pop in and out of what has to be another invisible dimension – a parallel reality. Another dimension that is 'stuck' to the underside of ours. This is like fabric that has gold thread woven into it that you can only see from one side. From our side we can't see the gold thread, but it is there, silently giving extra weight and support to the material. This invisible, unknown dimension might be like a giant spider's web that we can't see, but it extends out into the Universe, connecting everything up. A vibration at one end will send a rustle of energy down the web to all the other parts. So you put your toaster on and, somewhere out in the Cosmos, something 'knows'.

According to science, you have a dark super-body

There has to be something that gives matter its bulk and weight, or 'mass'. But according to physicists, the mass of the nucleus of an atom is far heavier that the sum of all its particles. That means if you add all the pieces together the total is more than it should be – a lot more! According to Nobel Prize winner, Frank Wilczek, 95 per cent more than it should be.[4] Amazingly, 95 per cent of an atom appears to be missing. We can only find or see 5 per cent. To explain this, there is a popular theory that states for every particle of matter in an atom there is an invisible particle of 'dark' matter called a 'super' partner.[5] All that seemingly empty space does have something in it that has mass or weight, but it is 'dark', which means it's invisible. This means we can't touch it, or see it, or interact with it. It doesn't weigh anything on our scales and it can't be measured with any scientific instruments that we've invented so far. And here's the really cool bit – because air is made up of atoms, and the particles in atoms have the dark super-partners, it's all around you now! Wave your hands around in front of you, (go on, no-one's looking!) and your hands are passing straight through it. It's right there with us, but we have no idea that it is, because it doesn't register with our senses.

This also means that you too have a 'dark' body, as well as the one you know about!

We know that we all have a mind, body, soul and spirit. Well, science is now proving the existence of these. The 4 per cent is our body and 96 per cent is our soul and spirit, which exists mostly in other dimensions, ones that are 'dark' or invisible to our material body. The mind is in both, with consciousness in the 4 per cent and unconsciousness in the 96 per cent.

What is the God particle?

There is one theory about a certain particle called a 'Higgs boson' or 'Higgs particle' that has captured the attention of many physicists, and it is believed that it may be responsible for much of the missing dark matter. It is named after Peter Higgs who was born in 1929. He wrote a physics papers in 1964, in which he theorised about the existence of a 'dark' energetic field pervading the Universe which drags on our real particles with it's own 'dark' particle, called the Higgs particle. When the Higgs particle drags on the particles in our atoms, it gives them the extra dark mass that we can't find.

For several years he was derided by his colleagues, but eventually the idea became the basis for lots of further development. However, it turned out that his career had peaked with that theory and he withdrew from cutting edge physics after that. He says "Because I'd written an influential paper, people tended to assume I understood far more about the subsequent theory than I did and I found it increasingly hard to keep up."[6] (I love that comment. This man is a Gemini who are known to be good at gathering knowledge but often derive no meaning from it.) The press dubbed the Higgs Boson the 'God' particle, but Higgs himself dislikes the term 'God' because he doesn't want to upset those who are religious.

A nine billion dollar experiment called the Large Hadron Collider

In order to get to the bottom of all this, scientists worldwide are working on the most ambitious experiment the human race has ever taken on. More ambitious even, than landing on the Moon. As I write this, we are witnessing the launch of a project involving the largest machine ever built, called the Large Hadron Collider (LHC), and its mission is to discover the Higgs particle, or any of the tiny, invisible particles of energy that may inform us of parallel universes and other dimensions. They have to find the dark particles in an atom, or the dark energy field to properly understand them. Scientists have caught tantalising glimpses of them in previous experiments with smaller machines, but now, paradoxically, to see even smaller, they need a bigger machine!

The LHC is a circular tunnel with a huge 27 kilometres long tube inside it, within which they can whirl beams of particles around. It is buried deep underground on the borders of France and Switzerland, near Geneva. It uses so much power that it can't be run over the Christmas holidays for fear of overloading the local electricity grid.[7]

To find the dark particles, scientists send beams of energy with particles of 'real' matter in them whizzing round inside the circular tube at the speed of light. After they have one beam whirling around they send another in the opposite direction and slam them into each other. Large detectors then measure the energy that is produced by the collision. Measuring the energy that is released tells them about the dark particles that were present, because there is a bigger dying energy signature than can be accounted for by the real matter.

This may seem like a lot of trouble to go to, but otherwise they would have to wait for these dark particles to pop in and out of our existence randomly, as they often do, but, like buses, they don't always turn up when expected!

Some of the statistics involving the LHC are mind-boggling. It involves scientists and support staff from 111 countries. It weighs 38,000 tonnes and its initial construction and manufacturing costs amounted to £3.5 billion. The beams of particles will travel at 11,000 circuits per *second*. The detectors in the ring are so sensitive they can feel the movement of the Moon as its gravitational pull sucks the water in the earth around the ring towards it, through up to 100 metres of rock! And lastly, part of it will probably be the coldest place in the Universe, at absolute zero degrees.[8]

Most of the matter out in space is missing too

Now it gets *really* interesting when we look at the matter out in the Universe, because dark and invisible happens on a much bigger scale. The fact is that 96 per cent of the known universe is missing and is made up of dark stuff.

Our Sun is one of at least 100 billion suns, all orbiting around a centre. This is called a Galaxy, and our Galaxy is called the Milky Way. When the scientists do the calculations to predict how much matter (suns, planets, clouds of gas) there should be in the Galaxy to stop it all flying apart, there is a lot missing. In fact, most of it is missing! In all, a staggering 96 per cent of the Universe is missing and called 'dark'.

Let me repeat that because it's just so amazing! When they add up the expected mass in the Universe, including all the galaxies, suns, planets and big clouds of gas and debris that exist in outer space, (including you, me and the cat!) it seems that 96 per cent of it is missing.

So just to sum up what we've got so far, 95 per cent of an atom is 'missing' and 96 per cent of the Universe is 'missing'. These two figures are close enough for us to assume that it is the same stuff that is missing or 'dark' in the very small (the microcosm) and the very large (the macrocosm).

Dark matter in the Universe

As far as the Universe goes, the experts have broken that down further and stated that of the missing 96 per cent, about 21 per cent is missing dark matter, and 75 per cent is missing dark energy. The remaining 4 per cent is our Universe as we know it, all the stars, galaxies, planets, Earth, you and me, the other six billion and *everything* else. The rest is an unknown Multiverse or dimension with possibly 11 other universes or dimensions in it.

So, as far as the Universe is concerned, two things are 'dark'. There is dark *matter* and dark *energy*. Dark matter accounts for 21 per cent of the Universe and it is everywhere you find real matter (your body, the Earth, the stars, etc.). It gathers around it in clumps. But it also stretches out into long filaments that cross the Universe and connect up stars and planets and galaxies in a super giant 'cobweb'.

It is only recently that we have had the means to detect all this, but by utilising the lastest technology scientists have produced images of it that you can find on the Internet. It looks exactly like cobwebs!

The latest research from an eminent scientist in the field says this:

> "We used to think that the vacuum was empty, and that objects
> were things in empty space. However, the vacuum is not
> empty. It is a medium. We are like fish in the ocean who regard
> water as empty space."

He also states that there may be up to 11 other dimensions and different worlds.[9] And before you suggest that he needs to take more water with it, he's not alone. One scientist at Fermilab states that "There are serious suggestions that new dimensions of space are opening up."

Dark energy in the Universe

So what is dark energy? God knows! And he's currently not telling. All the scientists know is that it is pretty evenly spread throughout the Universe. So there is as much in your bedroom as there is on the other side of our Galaxy. And it seems responsible for the fact that the Universe is still 'expanding'. Our Galaxy is growing at a rate of 80 kilometres per second.

The dark part of our own bodies, our soul and spirit, gets messages from the 96 per cent

It seems that science now agrees with the spiritual belief that messages come to us from out of the 96 per cent.

According to one scientist, the cells in our body are constantly receiving information from a higher organising authority or power, and some of it may come from the invisible web of connectedness. The cells in our body have an inbuilt receptive ability and they are also affected by changes in the electromagnetic waves around us.[10] Dr. Bruce Lipton, a biologist at the University of Wisconsin, agrees with him and states:

> "Hundreds of scientific studies… reveal that 'invisible forces' of
> the electromagnetic spectrum profoundly impact every facet of
> biological regulation."[11]

He says that that living organisms must receive signals in order to stay alive and that "specific frequencies and patterns of electromagnetic radiation regulate… all cellular behaviour that contributes to the unfolding of life."

Apparently these energy signals are a hundred times more effective that the chemical ones that our physical body relies on, such as the immune system or the endocrine system. This means that the energy that you invoke during reiki can be more effective than the body's own chemical healing system. He states that our beliefs and the energy waves we create in our thoughts create positive or negative responses. In other words, if we believe in something, this has an influence over our control of it. So if you and the patient believe in your power to heal, then your healing will be a hundred times more effective.

It is also known that a vast amount of nuclear power pours out of our Sun and constantly passes through our planet and bodies. The power comes in the form of quantum particles and some of these are called 'neutrinos'. Billions of them are passing undetected through our bodies all the time and it can take them as little as eight minutes to get from the Sun to our planet. The Sun doesn't just warm our bodies; it supplies an unseen spiritual sustenance. So we are all held together by an unknown energy or force that constantly feeds us with millions of signals. It is tempting to see this as being divine in nature. Almost certainly it comes out of the 96 per cent and the elements of fire and water are involved. In spiritual terms, we have ancient texts telling us that powerful forces guide us and everything on this planet. These were once called gods and goddesses and in my world planets such as Jupiter and the Sun represent them.

Some people are more connected to the invisible 96 per cent than others. These are the 'psychic' people, or those that just get 'gut' feelings that pay off with lucky events. Mediums and clairvoyants must all get their information from these other realms. Children especially are connected but as they get older they can tune it out. Ancient Hermetic texts talk of a silvery thread that connects a baby to the other realms and doesn't always get broken at the time of birth. It can remain connected for some time as the soul makes a decision to stay or return, or perhaps the soul needs the continued support of the soul lake in the 96 per cent for a while after birth. Eventually though, the thread is broken and the baby is 'earthed'.

An explanation simple enough for my mother to understand

If you found some of that heavy going, don't worry about it because it can take years to fully understand. You can always go back to it when you've read the rest of the book. Meanwhile, here is a simple explanation for now, which probably wouldn't pass as very scientific.

If you took a tiny cell from your arm and magnified it, you would not find a solid bit and the microscope would pass right through your arm. It looks solid and feels solid when it's all put together, but it is actually trillions of particles of spinning energy that gives the illusion of being solid. Like the spokes of a bicycle wheel that look solid when they are spinning, but allow you to see straight through when they have stopped. The spinning bits of energy in your arm have formed into a 'lattice' that holds together and repels things or feels resistant to touch. So when something touches it, both things feel solid. You are actually made entirely of energy and so is everything in the world around you.

The next important thing to know is that most of the Universe is 'missing' and here is a simple explanation for that.

Gravity pulls everything towards matter and holds on to it. Like the Earth holds on to us and the apple falls to the Earth. Gravity comes from matter or solidness and the Earth is a large solid lump so it has gravity which pulls us all into the centre. When scientists worked out how much solid stuff there would have to be in the Universe to keep everything in its place and stop it flying apart, they were puzzled to find that most of it is missing. In fact, 96 per cent is missing. It is there, but it is invisible to touch or measurement and we can walk right through it as if it wasn't there. The scientists call it 'dark'.

Everything that we know in our lives, all the planets, the Sun, the stars, our Earth and everything on it only add up to 4 per cent of the Universe.

This dark 96 per cent has other invisible realms in it that are in a different dimension. We can't pass into these other dimensions because our bodies are not vibrating at the right frequency, but other things such as magical healing power, spiritual guides and angels can.

We know we each have mind, body, soul and spirit. Our physical bodies are made of the matter of the 4 per cent, while the rest of us is the spiritual or etheric parts of our personality that exists in the 96 per cent. The soul and spirit in each of us move and exist in these other realms and this is how we can 'just know' things in our gut, communicate through psychic awareness, or 'read' cards.

These other realms contain things that we have became frightened of in the last 2,000 years but this is because we believed the horror stories of burning hell and purgatory told by the Catholic Church. They got the idea from volcanoes and it's not really like that at all. The ancient races that existed more than 4,000 years ago knew of and respected the other realms. To them they were simply the realms of the sky gods and the Underworld or Netherworld, which was where the Sun went at night.

As amazing as all that sounds it is absolutely true. We have always had proven scientific fact or theory mixed with spiritual teachings. Each of the coming chapters will refer to it again, so if you still don't understand it, don't worry because I'm sure you will do by the end of the book.

$$3$$

Ceres, Goddess of Growing and Grieving

4 *Ceres, a great Earth Mother goddess*

Ceres, the dwarf planet

Within the orbits of Mars and Jupiter there is a wide gap that has caused speculation since the 18th century. Astronomers of the time searched in vain for a planet that the laws of physics told them *must* be there Finally, in 1801 a planet the size of Texas was discovered in the gap and named Ceres, but as other objects were also discovered in the vicinity the area was given the title of asteroid belt and the newly named planet was demoted to being an asteroid.[1] Ceres's position in the sky was no longer reported on, so astrologers couldn't use her.

Then in the 1970s someone began to plot her position in the sky again and an astrologer wrote a book about her and the other planets in the asteroid belt.[2] Slowly, the astrological community was waking up to knowledge of the goddesses or planets that the asteroid belt contained.

In 2006 members of the International Astronomical Union met to decide what to call all the newly discovered planets of the 21st century, and their decision to create a new class of planets led to the surprise announcement that Ceres was big enough to join Pluto in being called a 'dwarf planet'. This meant that astrologers would start to use her, and that her energy was on the rise in the Collective.

Interestingly, in 2008, a report in *New Scientist* suggested that the planets Ceres and Pluto were once one body, or at least originated from the same place, in spite of the fact that there is a distance of up to four billion kilometres and four planets in between them. This report was highly significant, since these two are closely connected in mythology. As we shall see later, Ceres and her daughter Proserpine are two aspects of the same goddess although they are spoken of separately in the stories. Pluto is the brother of Ceres (called Demeter in Greece), but he also makes her daughter his queen and she rules the Underworld with him. The report entitled "Has Pluto sent us a message in Ceres?" says:

> "Does Pluto have a wayward cousin lurking in the inner Solar System? The dwarf planet Ceres… may have been born in the same realm as Pluto, but travelled all the way to the asteroid belt."[3]

Apparently the two planets are made out from the same material, and this doesn't occur anywhere else in the Solar System.

The Spiritual Meaning of Ceres

Putting it simply, Ceres represents the unconditional bond, nurturing and love between the source and the progeny, or the mother and child, and the 'rites of passage' that go with it. The growth of a seed into maturity, and then separation and preparation for re-birth. This might mean the cycle of human life from a seed to a baby, to a maiden, to a mother, or that of agriculture and grain in particular. Ceres is a symbol for separation and dying, and the mourning and grieving that goes with it, but she is also the energy that is with us as we prepare for re-birth, or a new beginning. The early civilisations believed that the human soul went through a cycle of death and re-birth just like the corn. Her myth is one of many concerning the death and re-birth of vegetation, and it exists to encourage us to believe that human life does not end in death.

Our soul is here to learn and grow, and it is a sad fact that sometimes the greatest growth is not without pain, because usually we have to see something end or pass before we grow into something new. Pain and spiritual growth are proportional to each other. Ceres comes to us not just for the light of birth, but also for the dark of death. She takes our hand and walks with us through the Underworld of the darkest of nights, and her gentle sensitivity teaches us of our soul and the reason for its existence. She tends us while we grow.

To explore her meaning more thoroughly, we first have to look at her myths, and then the energies that were prominent in the Collective when she emerged into our consciousness physically, as a newly discovered planet. Myths take us back to the goddesses, deities or energies of pre-history. These stories are as old as time, but very valuable because they have stubbornly survived oppressive religious or political dynasties. Some even look as if they *became* the basis for religious doctrine. When we need to understand something, it helps if we can look at the patterns, themes and issues in a context that we can comprehend. Because these myths have survived, we know that the human race must always have needed them, and that they must have found them rewarding. It's as if they remind us of some knowledge stored in our genes or our human DNA. They talk to or activate an ancient memory that we all carry deep inside us. Carl Jung, the psychiatrist, was convinced this was so.

The myth of Demeter and Persephone

Ceres was specifically introduced by the Italians to help deal with a drought in Rome in 496 BC, but she was originally known to the Greeks as Demeter or Earth Mother,[4] and going even further back, to the Ancient Egyptians as Isis. The best account of her myth is told in a hymn called "Homeric Hymn to Demeter" which was written in the 7th Century BCE and has several similar translations.

In a nutshell, the story describes the agony and mourning a mother (Ceres) goes through, when her daughter (Persephone) is abducted and taken into the Underworld to become queen and wife to the Lord of the Underworld. Eventually the daughter is returned when her mother withholds crops and food from the human Upperworld. The other gods cannot allow the human race to die, so they broker a deal that means the daughter will spend part of the year in the Underworld and part in the Upperworld. The object was to explain the mysteries of life and death, as it was forbidden to speak of them directly.

Here is a lengthy version of the story[5] which originally used the older Greek names of Demeter and Persephone throughout, but I've changed them to Ceres and Proserpine as the Romans did. It's helpful if you can remember both names for each, then when you read anything else you will know it is the same person. (That'll impress your friends!)

As the hymn begins, we find the two goddesses Ceres and her daughter, Proserpine, enjoying an idyllic day in a golden age of abundance and growth. Proserpine's father, Zeus, had decided that his brother Pluto would make a good husband for her, so it was agreed that the earth should split open and Pluto would rise up in his golden chariot and take Proserpine back into the Underworld with him. Strangely, although the Earth opened up to let Pluto abduct her, wherever he took her, Proserpine could still see the "star filled sky", the "fish-swarming sea" and the "rays of the Sun", so she had hope. The poem does not say how this was possible. I think it might be important for us to reflect on this detail. From the Underworld she could still see life on earth.

On the tenth day of searching, Ceres was helped by the goddess Hekate and the Sun god. Ceres refers to Proserpine as a "sweet young seedling" when asking of her whereabouts. This is making an important comparison between the growth of humans and plants. We can take from this that the two follow a similar cycle.

The Sun god said Pluto had taken Proserpine to the "misty realms of darkness". He urged Ceres to be pleased because Pluto was very high-ranking. Apparently Zeus, Poseidon and Pluto shared rulership of the known Universe. Ceres, however, was filled with grief over this. She then shunned the immortal world and decided to go and live as a human in a town in Greece called Eleusis, situated to the west of Athens. (It is interesting just how closely the world is interwoven between immortals and earthly mortals. They just blend into each other in the stories. Perhaps we are meant to understand how very close to us the gods are. However, goddesses must be tall, because we are told Ceres's head touched the ceiling.)

Ceres blessed four maidens with the wish that "you are able to bear children, in accordance with the wishes of your parents." (One of her main themes as a planet today is the area of childbirth and the bond between parent and child.)

Another of her themes is expressed when we are twice told that women say to Ceres "We humans endure the gifts the gods give us, even when we are grieving over what has to be." This goddess is very much involved with the grieving process of loss.

Ceres was then given the job of nanny to a late born, much wanted and treasured son of a King. She doesn't feed him breast milk or grain, but she raises him as a god. The act of eating symbolises engagement with the earthly realm. By not feeding, the baby does not become human. Every night Ceres placed the boy in the fire to burn any humanness from him, and this would have led to him becoming a god or divine spirit. (In astrology, fire is the symbol of spiritual understanding and deity. Ceres was feeding his soul with spirit.) The baby thrived and began to look like a god. He would have become ageless and immortal had his mother not discovered one night what Ceres was doing.

The mother screamed in terror at seeing her child in the flames and Ceres had to take him out of the fire and put him on the floor. Ceres was cross and said that humans were unable to recognise something fortunate. What looked bad now would have become something much better had it been allowed to go on. She could have made the boy immortal, but now he was doomed to die, as all humans must. This is another important point to grasp when considering what we can learn from the energy of Ceres. Although something may look tragic and terrible, in time and with persistence, something good can come out of it. Ceres insisted she is the "greatest boon and joy for immortals and mortals alike", and that contact with her gave something of value. However, it was only right that the young prince became human, and Ceres was forced to allow this.

Ceres then left instructions on how to perform the sacred rites that would teach the secrets of life and death (called the Eleusinian Mysteries), and at her bidding a temple was built.

Her grief and yearning for Proserpine continued and Ceres made it a terrible year for humans. The human race was near the brink of extinction and things were getting serious! If the human race died, then the gods would not be worshipped. Humans get their vegetation courtesy of the gods, but then the gods get something back from humans. Homage and adulation by humans is an act of focus that generates an energy or spirit which then passes into the ether and feeds the universal spirit of the 96 per cent. The gods desperately need this worship-generated energy, and it jeopardises their way of living if they don't get it. So Zeus intervened and instructed Pluto to let Proserpine go. Zeus ruled that she should spend a third of the year underground and two thirds in the company of Ceres and the other gods.

Ceres immediately filled the fields with a rich and bountiful harvest and all was well again. She then bestowed upon them her second great gift to the human race which were the Eleusinian Mysteries, the secrets of life and death.

The Eleusinian Mysteries and life after death, a guide into the Underworld

Ceres showed the mortals how to perform certain sacred rites and rituals associated with love. Whoever was initiated in these rites would "get a share of things" once they died and went into the "dank realms of mist". Once a human has seen these things they are sent "Ploutos or wealth personified, who gives riches to mortal humans".

They became the famous Eleusinian Mysteries and major 'initiation' or life and death rites of the ancient world. The Greeks believed that the soul of all growing things is in the earth and that the regeneration of spring after the death of winter is like the regeneration of the human soul after death. It was the common belief in Athens and Egypt that whoever had been taught the Mysteries would, when he died, be deemed worthy of divine glory. Hence all were eager for initiation.

Since Greek society at this time was moving towards masculine, or yang energy, *individual* importance and survival was becoming most important. Feminine, or yin energy, such as that of Ceres, tends to sacrifice single life in the knowledge that it is part of a whole which will be ultimately protective to the whole. As society became more focused on analytical self-development, it would have been inherently natural to maintain an appreciation of Mother Nature and Ceres as a kind of opposite to the prevailing cultural trend.

Probably to maintain the sacredness and importance, the exact content of these rites has remained a mystery, but we have a few clues.

In the hymn, Proserpine is referred to as a young seedling, and in fact the three goddesses named are all different manifestations or parts of the same cycle. The seed and young seedling (Proserpine), the mother plant bearing an ear of corn (Ceres), the withering plant after harvest (Hekate) and then the seed again. This can be translated into human seed, embryo, baby, maiden, mother, and so on. These are different stages of development of the same earthly process, that of life forms emerging, growing and decaying. It is likely that the Mysteries explained this.

In its simplest form, the myth explains the seasons. So when it talks of Ceres's mourning whilst Proserpine is underground, this could be a metaphor for Mother Nature mourning whilst the seed is underground, i.e. in the Underworld. This is the time when things must rest and go out of sight (death) before re-birth. This is the fundamental message of the Mysteries, that humans also share this cycle or pattern. Death is not a finality, it is a preparation for re-birth. The energy of Ceres is all about *growth*. How one life leads to another. How this year's crop provides the seed for next year after a period in the Underworld. A seed will always promise new life.

Another clue as to what happened in the Eleusinian Mysteries comes to us from pottery made around the time the hymn was written, and Ceres was introduced to Italy. A book on Athenian red figure vases[6] contains an example of a cup painted by an artist from Eleusis. This shows a male and female in an erotic act, which is apparently a rare scene for the time and may offer us some insight as to what was encouraged in the town of Eleusis!

Protector of life and death cycle, ensuring re-birth and growth

Ceres is a metaphor for Mother Nature in all her stages of growth and decay, and there is no doubt that Ceres is a symbol of life's evolution and generation through the physical process of nurturing seeds and harvests to fulfillment. Be it the human seed, as when we procreate and make a child, or seeds of grain. She has very strong associations with grains of corn in particular.

But Ceres is not only representative of the life and death cycle, she *protects* it. In the myth she could not stop Pluto or the Underworld taking her progeny for a while, *but* she did influence Proserpine's return. She simply did not allow there to be no re-birth, and her power proved to be the most influential. Let's reflect on that. She could not stop the death, but she *ensured* the re-birth. Ceres's greatest gift is that of growth, which we see when Proserpine was returned. The hymn tells us that the Earth was immediately filled with abundant fields of new corn. This is what she does best. She will stay, wailing and mourning with us during the loss, but always she seeks to grow. These days, Ceres guides souls into the Underworld, and out again.

The Freemasons state that Plutarch, a famous ancient Greek philosopher and initiate, says in his *Immortality of the Soul* that the soul at the moment of death, goes through the same experiences as those who are initiated into the great mysteries. The word and act are similar: we say 'telentai' (to die) and 'telestai' (to be initiated).[7]

Isis the Egyptian goddess

The myth of Isis, the Egyptian goddess, is almost identical. This time a young prince of Byblos is the child who is saved from mortal death by being engulfed in flames every night. When caught by the child's mother, Isis explained that she was burning away the mortal parts of the child so that he might live forever. However, the spell was broken so he would now die.

Isis is the wife and sister of Osiris, the mythical King of Egypt. Their brother, Seth, wished to rule, and murdered Osiris, scattering the body parts all over Egypt. Isis repaired the body sufficiently to draw semen from it with which she impregnated herself. She cared for the child, Horus, without her husband's earthly help, and brought him to his eventual position as a state god and mythical ruler of Egypt.[8]

In order to protect her son and assure his succession to the throne of Egypt, Isis had to accept that he be raised in secret by others, and so had to be separated from him for many years. Parent child separation and the parent child bond is one of her main themes.

After Isis used magic to resurrect him as a god, Osiris became ruler of the Underworld and King of Eternity and Isis became Queen of the Gods. She was also called "The provider of nourishment" and was the goddess of fertility and the harvest.

The ancient mysteries of Egypt

A very important event that happened around the year of Ceres's discovery was the invasion of Egypt by the army of Napoleon Bonaparte. He took with him a team of artists who published their famous work in 1801, the year of Ceres's discovery, and caused Egyptian antiquities to be 'discovered' too.

Paul Brunton was a guru and spiritual man who has been credited with bringing the experience and knowledge of enlightenment and spiritual awakening to the west.

In 1936 he wrote an extremely prophetic book,[9] which offered the following insights into the Egyptian Mysteries. He believed that the 'murder' of Osiris and his apparent resurrection in many of the wall paintings in the tombs of Egypt, was actually a depiction of the process of taking him into such a catatonic state that he appeared dead, but his awake and alive consciousness was in the next realm. In the book he describes what he felt actually happened:

> "The candidate was plunged by hypnotic means, involving the use of powerful fumigants as well as mesmeric passes the length of his body, combined with the use of a magically impregnated rod, into the death-like trance wherein he was deprived of every semblance of life. Whilst the body remained inert, the soul retained it's hold by a magnetic thread, visible to the clairvoyant initiator, so that vital functions were preserved despite the complete suspension of animation. The whole purpose... was to teach the candidate that there is no death. And he was taught this lesson... by dying and mysteriously entering another world

of being. When the allotted time of entrancement had elapsed he was re-awakened… thus the symbolic pieces of Osiris were put together and brought back to life." (pp169–173)

He goes on to tell us that the high priests were so adept at hypnotism and mesmerism that they could cause cataleptic conditions where even rigor mortis had set in. They knew how to keep the mind of the subject awake while his body was in this state, so he experienced paranormal events that were remembered after waking up. The priests wrote the "*Book of the Dead*" as guidance for these living dead people, whose soul was being initiated into another world. He continues:

"Although this process of initiation bore all the outward semblance of expert hypnotism, it was something that went far beyond the entrancement methods of our modern experimenters, who tap the subconscious mind of man but who cannot make their subjects conscious of still profounder planes of existence."

"…there was more philosophic doctrine and secret practice for the… spiritually educated and instructed Egyptians… the temples had special isolated buildings for the real Mysteries, which were performed by a select number of priests called hierophants."

"The greatest secrets… depended on the degree through which they passed. In the earlier degrees… they were made aware of their human soul, pictured as a small birdman in the hieroglyphs, and they had solved the mystery of death. They learned that it was really the disappearance of one state of being, before reappearing in another and that it affected the fleshly body, but did not destroy the mind or the self. They learned, too, that the soul not only survived the destruction of its moral envelope but progressed onwards to higher spheres."

"In the advanced degrees, they were made acquainted with the divine soul. They stood face to face with the Divine. They were first instructed in the true explanation of the fall of man from his original spiritual state. They were told the inner history of Atlantis. They were lifted up, sphere beyond sphere, until they found themselves in the same high spiritual consciousness as Man had enjoyed at the beginning."

Perhaps this was difficult for the local peasants to take, so simple stories involving myths and gods were used. Much later, the Greeks had watered down popular plays describing something similar. The ancient Egyptians wrote and painted their afterlife beliefs onto the walls of their tombs and onto papyrus. The most famous of these is the *Book of the Dead*.

The Egyptian Book of the Dead

The *Book of the Dead*[10] is a collection of the earliest spiritual and philosophical writings of humanity, and it tells us of the mysteries of life and death, giving advice to the souls of the living dead who go there. It was written thousands of years BCE and discovered in Egypt in the 1800s.

It seems to describe different 'planes of existence', 'hierarchies' or 'worlds' of afterlife or creation. Firstly in the creation, the great gods of the limitless primordial water and total darkness emerged out of non-existence. Then there came into being the celestial water, or celestial sky and stars, and the Duat or Underworld, in which Isis oversees a 'double gateway'. It appears we can travel to the Underworld or the Duat with help from Isis, and return with full knowledge of many spiritual things. Although this place is close to our own plain of existence, there are other deeper realms from which we can't return. The book confirms Isis as protector of the body-soul, or Ka, as opposed to the mind-soul, who is Nephthys, her sister, and states that Isis is "in charge of those who are to be examined".

There is one thing that caught my eye, and I include it only because it is amusing. In chapter 175, one god complains that the existence *beyond* the underworld has "no water, air, lovemaking, bread or beer, but (only) spirit being and contentment", which the Great Atum thinks he should be content with!

The return of the Great Goddess after an absence of over 1,000 years

As we have seen from all those representatives of the great Earth Mother, from Isis to Demeter to Ceres, this is a significant and important concept for our world. In all those millennia and those mighty civilisations, there was always a great Mother Earth goddess as a fundamental of life. Until the last 1,000 years or so, that is! Well, the Great Goddess is returning now and I for one am pleased to welcome her back.

Why will Ceres be important in the 21st century?

How Ceres's support will be needed in food supply after 2006

Ceres was introduced into Roman worship along with two older Greek deities in 496 BCE because the Italians were suffering drought and famine, and needed help.[11] Ceres must have been useful because six years later they built her a temple in the greek style, with priestesses of greek origin. She was designated a goddess of the working or common classes, which gave her nationwide appeal.

Ceres the planet was originally discovered at the beginning of an agricultural revolution caused by new ploughing methods devised in the early 1800s. She has very strong associations with grain in particular.

The sudden and surprising announcement of her elevated status to dwarf planet in 2006 could only mean that her energy was going to be keenly felt and much needed after that. We started to understand just how much in 2007, when it was announced by United Nations scientists that in order to feed the world's population, we would need to grow as much food in the next 50 years as we did in the last 10,000 years! The global population will rise from 4.4 billion in 1980 to an estimated 9 billion in 2050.[12]

From 2005 it became common to see gardening programmes on television that were entirely devoted to the growing of vegetables rather than gardening makeovers, and governments in the western world made impassioned pleas for people to not waste so much food.

There were food riots in third world countries as the price of staple grains trebled in a number of months. The changing climate conditions that brought about the loss of the world's food crops was not the fault of Ceres's, but was the work of Sedna. Ceres was actually helping to reduce the impact of the worsening weather conditions, as we found out in England in 2007, when she saved the potato and wheat harvest from failure due to flooding. Ceres was also introduced in Rome to assist with drought conditions, so she is useful for either!

The saving of the crops from the floods of 2007 was clearly shown in the astrology of the time. Both Sedna and Neptune were flooding large parts of England and the situation looked dire. Then slowly the planet Ceres edged in front of Sedna, and stood between Sedna and the Earth, halting her influence. Within hours the rain stopped. The fields dried out, and the harvest could be brought home. The image of how Ceres did this still brings tears to my eyes, it is a shame that at the time so few of us knew of her brave and timely protection.

Growing babies, child abduction or separation and Madeleine McCann

The terror of abduction is something that mothers in the 21st century will identify with most readily. The abduction of Madeleine McCann in May 2007 was reported worldwide. No one will forget the terrible sadness that we all felt. Madeleine's horoscope shows a very strong connection with Ceres, and there was a very significant Ceres energy involved on the day of her abduction. During 2007 and afterwards,

Kate and Gerry McCann were on a global stage, expressing all the grief, anguish and mourning which Ceres suffered in the myth.

Ceres, cycles and the passage of time

Ceres gives us an understanding of nature, her cycles and the passage of time, including patience!

When she was introduced to the Italian peasants, it was made clear that she was a goddess for the plebians. The daily work of the farming community revolved around the natural calendar. There was a yearly plan and it could not be hurried. Sowing, weeding and harvesting were all at set times of the year, and this gave the working classes stability, routine and order. They had to stay with their land. This teaches patience and an acceptance of the dominance of a greater will than our own. Ceres says the 21st century is the time to re-learn this skill!

Ceres supports us through death and bereavement

The terrible pain of the loss of a loved one is an awful and tragic experience. But somewhere on that wretched journey there is a point at which the bereaved desperately want to know why. And maybe understanding an individual loss in the context of the great cycle of life can in time offer some solace, as we then understand that the soul of our loved one is only out of sight for a while. They will return to live again, and this is promised to us by the presence of Ceres. Her rites show us a better way to understand what death and the Underworld is really all about. Maybe, if we understand that there will be a re-birth, we can find it more bearable.

A significant difference in our culture is our fear and horror of the perceived atrocity of the Underworld. The ancient Greeks had no such conception, or at least it is not a feature of the ceramics of the time. It was the Catholic Church that would introduce the horrors of a place of burning hell fires and purgatory. No such place existed for the ancient Greeks.

5 *Illustration of
the Underworld
on a Greek vase*

This illustration of a vase from ancient Greece shows a rare scene
of the Underworld with the winged souls of the dead filling a giant
container with the individual waters of knowledge from their own
vessels. It is a calm and peaceful scene. A single figure is shown to the
right, toiling uphill with a large rock; perhaps an illustration of life, and
what it took to get the waters of knowledge! According to a professor of
archaeology[13] these black figure vases give a valuable picture of life in
Greece at the time and "the Underworld held little interest."

We live our lives enduring pain and enjoying happiness. As the *Book
of the Dead* points out, we must drink, eat and make love. As we do
this, our soul is constantly gathering experience and wisdom. When
we die, our soul, spirit and mind return to their separate 'homes'. The
soul joins the Collective soul and pours into it all the wisdom and
experience it has learnt. Some pour for longer than others!

Does it help the bereaved to understand the context in which their
loved one has passed on? I like to think so. It can be understood that
their death contributes to a cycle of life in which they continue to play
a major role. That single life is not meaningless, but continues to have
great value.

Another way of looking at this is to see Proserpine, Ceres and the Old
Crone as simply extensions of each other. Different stages of the same

energy. There is no 'individual', and so no 'individual' death. We are all connected. Life flows through the generations that are born from each other.

Pindar said "Happy is he who, having seen this, goes beneath the earth. He knows the end of life and he knows its god-sent beginning".[14]

Certainly, as the years unfold after Ceres's 2006 revival there will be a changing attitude to death and its circumstances. The National Health Service and Marie Curie Foundation have recently launched a joint initiative to open up discussion between the dying and their survivors, so that fear and taboo will not prevent the death rites being as respectful and honourable as possible.

Previously, our taboo and discomfort at talking about and accepting the imminent death of someone close meant that their dying moments were in a resuscitation unit, far from the gentle hands of their loved ones, as medics vainly tried to hold back the inevitable tide of death. I think Ceres will slowly introduce us to the idea of letting loved ones go with dignity and peace. Home birth has become an aspiration, and now home death needs to be as well!

Ceres and the parent-child bond

In astrology, Ceres is the symbol of the parent-child bond. She is as much about the care and nurturing we give our progeny, as she is about the farmer's care and nurturing, which gives a good harvest of wheat.

In the early 21st century, it is likely that we will all experience the issues within a parent/child relationship as Ceres makes herself known. In this first decade alone, many have struggled with strong mother/daughter, control/breaking free psychological issues.

Carl Jung said "Every mother contains her daughter in herself and every daughter her mother. Every woman extends backward into her mother and forward into her daughter."

This will be hard for some daughters to accept, and yet it is true that daughters carry the epigenes, spiritual and soul inheritance of the whole maternal family lineage. The matriarchal energy is passed on from mother to daughter, generation after generation. So, yes, you *are* your mother!

A few might have experienced more profound sorrow or grief at separation from a parent or child, and for these unfortunate souls, reflection on the deeper meaning of Ceres may bring some understanding or comfort.

Other Ceres issues can include family misunderstandings, revengeful or devouring mothers, or the isolation of being alone with a child.

Some final thoughts

"To enter into the figure of Ceres means to be pursued,
to be robbed, to be raped, to fail to understand, to rage and
grieve, but then to get everything back and be born again."

Carl Jung [15]

If there is one theme that I feel is the reason for our lives here on earth, then it has to be that we should know and understand ourselves better. Unfortunately this is also one of the hardest things to achieve! To help us however, we have been given pain. For it is when we are in pain that we achieve the greatest growth towards the goal of knowing ourselves. We wouldn't bother otherwise.

There is no greater love on earth than that of a mother for her child. When this love takes us to our own 'underworld' of death and humility while we are still living, then we are truly in the greatest pain known to mankind. A personal hell on earth.

Surely then, this is when the strangest of things can happen. We grow. Our soul grows. We can experience a side of ourselves that would be unknowable otherwise. We see our soul, and the reason for its existence. The darkest hour has the greatest light. And Ceres takes our hand. She walks with us and tends us while we grow.

PLUTO, LORD OF THE INVISIBLE REALMS

6 *A seated Pluto, his wife Proserpine, Hermes holding the caduceus and a mortal*

So where has Pluto gone to?

In 2006 an announcement from the IAU said that Pluto had been demoted and was no longer a planet in our Solar System. Where had it gone then? Well, of course the planet itself hadn't gone anywhere, but it would not be *called* a 'planet' anymore. It was now a dwarf planet of the Kuiper Belt.

In astrology, this planet symbolises overwhelming and threatening change that challenges the old order of things and brings about evolution and transformation with power being lost or gained. So the announcement of the changes to Pluto, and the response from the public, was entirely consistent with the astrological meaning of Pluto, and as a Collective we reacted in the way that people usually respond when faced with the challenge that Pluto represents. Some embraced the change easily, some felt real loss and others tried to cling to the old order by refusing to acknowledge the new regime. However, the Pluto experience means that things can never go back to the way they were before, and likewise the changes to our Solar System remained.

In the same way that we need to look for the silver lining when having a personal Pluto experience, we also need to look at how re-categorising the planets can symbolise Collective growth and enlightenment. If our perceptions of Pluto the planet are undergoing revelation and change, then so will the human race undergo metamorphosis and a different way of being.

In this chapter, I am going to cover what the Pluto dominated changes will be about. Putting it in a nutshell, we will gain knowledge, and we will come to be less fearful. We will fear death less, we will fear the Underworld less, we will fear magic and miracles less, we will fear the secret power of the unconscious less, we will fear sub-atomic and nuclear power less, we will fear change less. Quite a list! But first we have to let go of some stuff! Such things as taboos and 2,000 years of brainwashing by religious dynasties. Old scientific certainties such as the molecular structure of matter and how many planets there are in the Solar System will all have to go.

The mythology and ancient stories of Pluto

Pluto as ruler of the Underworld in Roman and Greek mythology

According to *Bulfinch's Mythology*, Pluto and his two brothers ruled over three dominions. Jupiter (Zeus) was the father of gods and men and ruled the sky and heavens, Neptune (Poseidon) ruled the oceans, and Pluto ruled over the realms of the dead, which included the infernal regions and Tartarus. They were often referred to as the Underworld, and the land of the mortals was sometimes referred to as the Upperworld. Earth and Olympus were common property.[1]

The realms of the dead could be accessed in different ways and Pluto had a throne and a palace which he shared with his wife, Proserpine. Pluto *regulated* the amount of souls in the different regions, and we are told in one story that he intervened to stop Aesculapius when he became so proficient at healing that he learned how to bring the dead back to life. Pluto would not allow this; only he and his queen were allowed to dictate what became of those souls who must accept the birth and death cycle and pass through the realms of the dead.

Another of Pluto's concerns was to ensure that his realm did not become exposed to the Upperworld, and he would check that it remained invisible by travelling around it in his carriage.

One of the most important myths concerning Pluto is that of Ceres and Proserpine, which can be read in detail in the previous chapter.

The story of Adam and Eve in the Christian Bible

There is another myth that is not so commonly associated with Pluto, but I feel it demonstrates another facet of this energy, which we need to understand in our dealings with him. Again, it shows how innocence can never be recovered, how things *must* change and move on.

It is the story of Adam and Eve in the book of Genesis.[2] We are told that God made Adam and Eve and a beautiful garden that housed, amongst other things, the Tree of All Knowledge. God forbade them to eat the fruit from this tree, warning that it would open their eyes to right and wrong, good and bad, and the ability to distinguish between the two. They would then be doomed to die. A serpent appears, tempting Eve into picking the fruit and sharing it with Adam. The supernatural, powerful and 'dark' realms are often symbolised by the serpent.

All this resonates very clearly with the Pluto theme and its associated Zodiac sign of Scorpio in astrology. As with the Ceres myth, we see the intervention of Pluto energy in Eve's life causing an action that has life or death consequences and makes irrevocable changes to innocence. Sexual activity, temptation, regeneration, magic, lust, jealousy, the occult and the serpent itself are all ruled by the astrological sign of Scorpio and this story contains all of these things. But obviously, these natural laws must exist because the tree was there in the first place! If God really didn't want to risk having his perfect creations contaminated by the changes that this tree could cause, why have the tree there? This must have been unavoidable, since it would obviously have suited him to *not* have it there. This seems to indicate that the Scorpionic power and natural law, which says all must be part of a cycle of transformation and change, is unavoidable, even for God.

Back to the story! The couple are banished from the garden with various punishments. Adam shall toil hard with farming, then die and be buried in the earth, and Eve shall suffer the intense pain of childbirth. (Eve means 'life giving' in Hebrew.) The serpent looses his wings and is made the enemy of womankind. Why just womankind?

Well, maybe because the serpent represents Pluto, and Pluto is all about the procreation of the species, and how this impulse is more powerful than individual life. It dominates supremely. Because woman takes the more active role in procreation by actually having the new life grow inside her, and then giving birth to it, it is more so the woman than the man who has to experience the danger of childbirth, and try to maintain personal power when her offspring and husband require her to meet their needs unconditionally for many years. The Bible says that God's punishment also includes welcoming a husband's affections and his mastership over her.

The riches that can be gained from this are evident when the woman then grows very strong as a result of her ability to 'take the weight'. If the traditional roles of 'woman at home', and 'man out at work' are followed, as the Bible seems to indicate here, then I believe the woman learns a tremendous amount about herself (and her own mother), as she hears herself repeating the things she swore she never would when she was a child! Having children, and seeing ourselves being raised to the ground and rebuilt (which is what child rearing does), is probably the *most* important contribution to our own self-development. More than in any other important relationship, our children hold up a mirror for us to see ourselves. This is transforming.

Let us reflect for a moment on the different attitudes to sex found in the texts upon which whole religious dynasties are based. Pluto/Scorpio is the energy in astrology that represents sex, as part of our procreation and the life and death struggle to keep our souls evolving. (Let's face it, if sex stopped, the human race wouldn't last for very long!) Although the Bible was rewritten from ancient texts that originated elsewhere in the Middle East, it completely changes earlier documentation on this matter. In the Corpus Hermeticum Asclepius texts there is reference to childbirth and great it is, with the inference that *celibacy* will earn punishment by the daimones after death.

The God of the Bible, on the other hand, *promotes* celibacy and all that is chaste, pure and untouched. However, Scorpio/Pluto took over in the guise of the serpent, and when Adam and Eve ate the fruit they became "evil" and took part in sexual intercourse and pleasures of the flesh. This is interesting because they now needed to.

Before they ate from the tree they were not human, they were immortal, so they didn't need sex, procreation or children, because like angels, they would never have to replace themselves. The fruit of the tree removed that immortality however, and their lives were then limited. So they then needed to procreate to keep the human race going.

Siva the destroyer and transformer

The Pluto energy of astrology has great resonance with the god Siva or Shiva of the Hindu religion, and although there is no recorded mythological connection between this god and the planet, it is just too obvious to ignore and one or two present day astrologers have made this connection.[3] However, Indian mythology is complicated so apologies if this interpretation hasn't quite captured all the nuances. If ever you have a spare decade or two, try reading the *Secret Doctrine* by Helen Blavatski written in 1888. She wrote extensively about the Creation, using a rich source of religious and mythical texts, and although her text is jumbled and rambling, it was way ahead of its time. Helen has this to say of Siva:

> "Siva… is the destroyer, as Vishnu is the preserver; and both
> are the regenerators of spiritual as well as of physical nature.
> To live as a plant, the *seed* must die. To live as a conscious
> entity in the eternity, the passions and senses of man must die
> before his body does. 'To live is to die and to die is to live' has
> been too little understood in the west. Siva, the *destroyer*, is
> the *creator* and the saviour of spiritual man, as he is the good
> gardener of nature."[4]

You might need to get a glass of wine and read that again! It means that Siva brings an end to earthly experiences so that we focus on our spiritual side. This and other texts are also saying that everything created must also contain the energy and potential of destruction. Everything must have a beginning and an end. What came into existence must return to non-existence, or the 'qualityless immensity'. This profound thought was part of the most ancient Indian texts. Putting that into the context of this discussion on Pluto, it means that what comes out of the Underworld and into the Upperworld, what is born, must eventually whither and die, with the soul returning to the Underworld.

The religious texts discussing Siva say that existence is only a stage in the expanding universe as it heads for ultimate destruction. Siva heads towards disintegration, and nothing can escape this process of destruction. He is the power of disintegration, and he alone remains in the beginning and the end.[5]

One of Siva's less aggressive titles is Lord of Sleep, and he has a huge influence over the practice of yoga, where one tries to attain the ultimate in transcendence and peaceful stillness. The 'sleep' title is interesting, as it isn't immediately obvious how this fits in with the destroyer image. However, it becomes clearer when Helen Blavatski refers to a period of sleep, silence and inaction during the chaos of the Creation.

In the '*Myths and Gods of India*', we are told that when things are depleted, or a human is tired, they enter into Siva, which is sleep and the changeless state. This is a joyful abode, where they can rest. Thus the everyday state of painless sleep or meditation is said to be the closest experience we can get to the peaceful non-existence of the next dimension, the place our soul will go when this human form is worn out and expired. The Underworld.

> "We fear death that is eternal sleep because of our failure to understand its significance. Man, in his world of illusion, fears death, even though it means for him liberation from bondage, all that is to be desired."[6]

Our fear of death is seen as ignorance, while the wise will see Siva as 'auspicious' and the 'ambrosia of all joy'. Apparently, entering into the highest state of Siva should be the supreme goal of an Indian yogi.

The rise and rise of our fascination with ancient Egypt

Another civilisation that had a highly developed sense of another realm that intertwined with ours was the ancient Egyptians. An Egyptologist says that:

> "…judging solely from the decorations on the walls of their tombs, many of which show the daily activities of the

Egyptians, they enjoyed life to the full. It would seem that their preparations for death owed much to their wish to perpetuate that enjoyment."[7]

"In order to reach the afterlife, the dead had to face a perilous journey through the Duat. The Duat is sometimes translated as Hell of Hades, but these terms convey ideas that were alien to the Egyptians, and it perhaps safer to translate Duat as the Underworld."[8]

The Duat was only as far away as the night, and the Sun travelled through it every night. It was just like Egypt, with the short cycle of night and day being a metaphor for the longer cycle of birth and death. Once again we are given obvious examples of how a civilization knew without doubt that there was a parallel universe where souls went to, but would definitely return from, if given specific instructions. These instructions are like the scientific understanding or mathematical equations that we will need.

Their belief in the Underworld went a lot further than present mainstream western thinking, where we just vaguely hope that there might be something more when we die. They totally accepted the existence of two realms, and these were represented by the obvious distinction between night and day. So they accepted that life has a 'dual' nature. There are 'dual' realms. There is a book, written by an enlightened Egyptologist, called *Serpent in the Sky*,[9] which seeks to prove that the snake or serpent, which is so prevalent in Egyptian art, is dedicated to the theme of duality. Seth, a god associated with the Underworld is also associated with the scorpion and the serpent, strong symbolism with the Pluto theme that I am examining here. The Egyptians understood that the two worlds were intertwined, and now science has actually accepted the presence of another invisible dimension that exchanges energy with ours. They say it consists of 'dark' matter and 'dark' energy; a term ancient spiritual texts always used when discussing the Underworld. It seems strange to now be able to point to the recent scientific evidence of the quantum realm and state that there *is* another dark dimension intertwined with ours and the Egyptians were right all along. The scientists have proved that energy moves from the other dimension into ours and out again, so it makes complete sense to me that the human soul and spirit is able to do likewise when we die or perhaps even when we sleep.

Egyptian god Ptah "he who made all and created the gods"

An ancient Egyptian stone tablet, called the Shabaka stone, carved with text that may have originated from the period betwwn 3100 and 2686 BCE, gives a great deal of insight into the almighty creator god of Ptah. It is stated by an eminent Egyptologist[10] that the doctrine of Ptah came from the beginning of Egyptian history, and that he is the oldest god, being the creator of everything else. The tablet is particularly interesting because it is written in an unusual back to front and mirror image way. It has very ancient glyphs, but a sophisticated grammar, leading some experts to believe that it *could* have been influenced by a very ancient master race. Whether or not we take the text on the tablet to have Atlantean origins, it has been called "the most remarkable monument of Egyptian thought which we possess."[11]

The Shabaka stone tells us that Ptah is the energy of creation and that he is everywhere and in everything, and that he is above (celestial) as well as below (terrestrial). All the other gods and everything else came into being at the behest of Ptah and he created the gods (energies) that are in all types of organic matter. This is incredible knowledge since we now know that all matter is actually made up of tiny particles of spinning energy. Everything is content and united under him, and Mother Nature is infused with the sustenance and energy that comes out of the two lands which he unites.

It appears from this text and many other sources that Egypt was once two separate lands, Upper and Lower Egypt, and although this may be the case, this could also be a metaphor for the two dimensions of Underworld and Upperworld, or for our dimension and the parallel invisible universe that science has now proven exists. Apparently, Ptah holds the balance between the lands of Underworld and Upperworld, and this resonates with the much later Greek myth of Pluto, where we are told that he regulates the number of souls in the Underworld.

Interestingly we are also told that Ptah's heart and tongue were used in the Creation. This is unusual, as it is a way of saying that *thought* was behind the Creation. This is the earliest known text that suggests that thought, or a divine intelligent plan, is behind creation. That it wasn't just spontaneous combustion but an intellectual concept underpinning life, a Universal Mind.

The goddess Tiamat from the Sumerian Tablets of Creation

Around 6,500 years ago, in the area now known as southern Iraq, a master race sprang into existence. They gave us writing, the wheel, engineering, mathematical and scientific knowledge, sophisticated cities and law. They were called the Sumerians, and it seems they passed on their knowledge to all the great dynasties that came after them. The Greeks and the Christian Bible copied much of their literature. One of their greatest legacies is a set of baked clay tablets called the Seven Tablets of Creation, or the 'Enuma Elish'. This story describes an image of primordial feminine, the first Great Mother of existence or Mother Nature. Whilst she is an *image* of primordial feminine she is also *the* primordial feminine, and she is called Tiamat. It may seem strange that I am writing of a female energy to describe Pluto, but after many years of studying Pluto's effect on us, I have no doubt that Pluto can best be described as the dark feminine as opposed to the dark masculine. A few thousand years ago major civilisations started to make all the spiritual figureheads masculine, and by the time of the Greek empire around 500 BCE, women and the feminine were subjugated and devalued to a very low rank. Important feminine had been replaced with important masculine, but there is no reason now to continue this unnatural state of affairs. The emergence of the dwarf planets in astrology symbolises the end of this era, and the re-emergence of the feminine, so maybe god*dess* can now take back some of the important spiritual positions.

According to a translation of these clay tablets by Leonard W. King in 1902, Tiamat "hath spawned monster serpents". (Note the serpent connection again.) She was "sharp of tooth and merciless of fang. With poison instead of blood she hath filled their bodies. Fierce monster-vipers she hath clothed with terror". None could withstand them, and vipers, dragons, raging hounds, mighty tempests and scorpion men are all mentioned.

All this really does give a wonderful image of savage, raging, wrathful chest-beating vengeance, and if you talk to any ex-husband about his ex-wife after a Pluto transit has seen them through a vicious divorce case, he will use similar words! Likewise the rejected femme fatale in the movie '*Fatal Attraction*', where she boiled the family bunny to get her own back. Some of Pluto's endings can be very vengeful and bitter with all manner of raging jealousy and vicious attacks. This is the dark side of feminine and Pluto.

Tiamat is eventually killed by her son, who was called Marduk, who who represents masculine energy and the civilised human race. A metaphor for how the masculine conquered the feminine, and how humanity's civilised side has conquered our primeval one.

The Sumerian (Iraqi) goddess called Ereshkigal

The Sumerians also had a goddess of the Underworld called Ereshkigal, and some well preserved clay tablets give us a story which is useful to us if we want to consider what the new image of Pluto is all about.

Ereshkigal has a sister called Inanna who must visit her in the

Underworld, (perhaps something to do with a lover). After passing through seven gates and being stripped of clothing and adornment at each one, Inanna eventually kneels naked before Ereshkigal. She is then unceremoniously hung on a meat hook to die. However, a previously hatched escape plan meant that she is saved and emerges from the Underworld again with praises and thanks for Ereshkigal.

To understand this myth, we first have to understand what Inanna represents. In astrology, Inanna, (the planet Venus) represents our self-esteem and self worth and what we should seek for ourselves to give ourselves affirmation and self satisfaction. She tells us about our choices in relationship too, what we need to give ourselves to get that 'wow!' factor. What we find attractive and beautiful, how we desire someone. This is part of our personality, part of our ego.

So the myth shows us that romantic relationships can take us into our own personal Underworld, and if we take the Underworld as a metaphor for having a terrible and humbling experience, such as the loss of a loved one or relationship, then it is clear that the myth is meant to comfort us by pointing out that we can emerge from the suffering. Although we are told at the beginning of this myth that no one ever emerges from the Underworld, it is clear they do, since Inanna does, and this gives a lesson of great value.

Having determined to get out of the Underworld, we can make the best of our lives, and these myths promise us the riches of command, mastery and wisdom as a result. We emerge battered but triumphant, humbled but stronger. It reminds me of the saying "We don't lose when we get knocked down, we lose when we *stay* down." Pain and gain are directly proportional to each other, so the greater the pain, the greater the potential for gain, although it may not seem like it at the time!

Further evidence that this whole myth is a metaphor for humbling experiences can be found in the few images we have of Ereshkigal. She is often shown controlling a lion, which represents our ego, potency and strength (Leo in astrology). When we go into our darkest personal Underworld of hell, it is our ego and will that is being tamed.

It is humbling to think that a myth written 6,000 years ago has survived to advise us that the suffering and humiliation we may receive in our darkest hours of hell on earth in the Underworld can be good for us. And that we may grow stronger and wiser as a result.

Ereshkigal herself is painted as a desperate, lonely and grieving figure. She longs for a sexual relationship and the companionship of a mate. If Ereshkigal is taken as a metaphor for the Underworld and Pluto, then we witness Pluto's craving and desperation for life-giving, procreative and therefore comforting, sexual fulfilment. This serves to remind us that relationships themselves can take us into the Underworld, but so can lack of one! There are those of us whose lives are a misery without a relationship and sexual fulfilment. Since Pluto's power is transformative and definitely creative, we should remember that we all have the potential to create a life-changing relationship.

The meaning of Pluto in astrology

The discovery of Pluto the planet

Events around the discovery of any planet tell us something of its meaning, so we need to look at Pluto's.

Pluto was discovered in 1930 and was considered for many years to be the farthest planet from our Sun, and certainly the smallest, at only 70 per cent the size of our Moon.

But in the early 1930s science was also getting 'smaller' with breakthroughs in sub-atomic science, the splitting of the atom, and the theoretical discovery of an unknown, invisible force or dark energy that made up two thirds of the Universe. As we know, in the early years of the 21st century this was finally proven to exist, just as Pluto hit the headlines again for being re-designated a 'dwarf' planet.

The scientific breakthroughs of 1932 have been referred to as the "miracle year" of British physics[12], but the science was so hard to understand and explain, the journalists and public gave a yawn and turned to the sports page!

Plutonium was then manufactured and named after Pluto in 1941 and this new scientific discovery eventually led to an atom bomb being dropped on Japan. Destruction on this scale was too much to contemplate, and the human race turned away from atomic power.

The traditional meaning of Pluto in astrology

In astrology we understand that Pluto is an agent for transformation and change and represents evolution and the evolutionary force. The word 'evolution' means unrolling and unfolding, a gradual change over successive generations. It's also about expansion through enlargement and development. To evolve means to disclose, to progress and to mature. If you look back on that list, you will see there are some encouraging words there!

Pluto is an intelligent, ever present, ruling principle in the universal life force which fulfills the cycle of evolution without restraint or sympathy. It is built into the very structure of life. If necessary, there will be a fight to the death, but it doesn't matter, because Pluto knows there will always be re-birth, and ultimately life will always emerge. So although the destruction may be great, this should be seen in the light of the need for constant improvement, a maturing and progressive force.

The Pluto energy describes life, death and re-birth in a never-ending cycle. It is a principle of regeneration, relentless growth and purging; an underlying code in which the rules of nature are written. Pluto ends that which has outlived its usefulness, sometimes in a remorseless way, but although the immense power might end the chapter and turn the page, Pluto also brings new life. This power never ceases to create.

According to astrologer Linda Goodman the sacred number for this planet is zero, which represents power. She points out that we add a zero to numbers to increase their power, and the more zeros we add the more powerful something becomes.[13]

In ancient astrology, the circle represents the incomprehensible absolute unity and presence of all life. It is everything, for example, the dark and the light. The source of all, it is present in all, it existed before our Solar System, and it will exist after it has disappeared. This thing-that-can't-be-understood has no space or time limits.[14]

Pluto has a strong association with the Zodiac sign of Scorpio. The Zodiac is simply the sky or Universe around the Earth divided up into twelve portions. Let's say you are standing at the centre of a cake; the Zodiac refers to the 12 wedges of cake that fan out around you. The part of sky called Scorpio is associated with Pluto and there are many similarities between the sign and the planet.

Scorpio also represents things that are buried and hidden, including deep knowledge, psychology and the secret power of the unconscious. It has associations with magnetic attraction, sexual activity and lust, which are all bound up with the theme of procreation. Sexual union holds the potential to experience the intense currents of the great creative and generative force.[15] When two people are joined there is a potential for transformation on a soul level, as well as the potential to actually create new life. Sexual attraction and desire is a strange and mysterious thing that holds huge emotional energies, and Scorpionic people want to experience the crisis and euphoria of deep emotional exchange. These feelings create powerful urges and instinctive primal reactions, which can toss victims into their own personal underworld of feelings and hell if it all goes wrong.

Pluto and the number nine

"Plato regarded geometry as sacred, the Pythagoreans declared 'All is number', and the heading of the Egyptian Rhind Papyrus promises rules for enquiring into nature and for the knowing all that exists, every mystery, every secret."[16]

During the course of this project, curious co-incidences arose that featured the number nine.

A space mission, launched in 2006 to explore the Pluto family, will take nine years to get there, arriving in 2015.

One of the recently discovered moons is called Hydra, a mythical beast with nine heads, and the name was chosen with regard to Pluto's position as the ninth planet.[17]

A team of nine astronomers found two new moons, Nix and Hydra.[18]

In 1888, when only eight planets were known to exist, Helen Blavatsky wrote a book about science, religion and philosophy called *The Secret Doctrine*, in which she stated that the ancient initiates of Vishnu knew of more than seven planets. "Parasara speaks of the chariots of the *nine* planets which are attached by aerial cords to the Pole Star."[19]

According to the Egyptian Shabaka stone, Ptah gave birth to the nine Neters or chief deities of Egypt.

A man called Geoff Stray reported on a television programme in 2009 that nine was also important to the Mayans, who predicted that 2012 would see the return of the Nine.

What does all that mean?

According to astrologer, Linda Goodman,[20] nine represents 'material life' and the beginning and end of life on the material plane of existence. Multiplying cannot destroy nine and this is true of no other number.

For instance: $2 \times 9 = 18$ then add $1 + 8$ and you get 9

$3 \times 9 = 27$ then add $2 + 7$ and you get 9

$14 \times 9 = 126$ add $1 + 2 + 6$ and you get -9!

This gets more interesting when she describes how nine gives life back to each of the single numbers.

For instance: 9 plus 1 = 10 1 plus 0 = 1 again

9 plus 2 = 11 1 plus 1 = 2 again

9 plus 4 = 13 1 plus 3 = 4 again

There are more examples of these, but her point is that nine is the king of numbers, the sacred number of eternity, and the entire edifice upon which human life on this planet is based. This is comforting since it cannot be destroyed!

In astrology, nine represents conflict, strife and the ability to penetrate. This meaning is compatible with the effect the planet tends to have on people. The actual planet of Pluto has the number of zero, but I think the additional message of 'nine' energy, which seems important at this time, gives us another layer of meaning to contemplate. Let's look again at Linda Goodman's words. The number nine represents material life, and the beginning and ending of this life. Material life is all the 'matter', the planets and stars, our Earth, the whole human race and everything that we can see or feel.

In his book, *Serpent in the Sky*, J. A. West states that the number nine is extremely complex. Nine emanates from the absolute divine; it is "interpenetrating, interacting and interlocked." So it's like the fabric or matrix of interwoven existence. In recent years science has become obsessed with finding the origins of life. Billions of pounds are being spent on sophisticated instruments dedicated to a single focus – what's the theory of everything? The single equation that will give a provable, undeniable paper explanation. The two frontiers of exploration, the immensity of space, and the sub-atomic, are coming together in an effort to get *the* answer. The emphasis on the number nine surrounding Pluto is a reflection of this.

The serpent as a symbol of healing and magic

There are two symbols in common use by the medical profession featuring serpents coiled around a staff. One shows a single serpent, and the other is the caduceus, which shows *two* serpents! Medical organisations throughout the world proudly display these symbols.

"The serpent upon the staff was quite universally the symbol among the ancients of the medical art. The serpent signified the principle of occult life, and the staff or rod was the symbol of magic power."[21]

Astrology has always understood Scorpio's rulership over healing and the healing arts, and this won't cause a problem to most people. But Scorpio also rules magic and the occult, and this is something that the medical profession certainly doesn't want to be associated with! Certain associations in America are now trying to disassociate from the caduceus, or two serpent version, because it is linked to Hermes, the Greek God who is associated with the Hermetic texts and secret doctrine.[22] This, they say, is paganism, witchcraft and magic... and astrology. My, my, how awful. The Hermetic texts were copied from even earlier documents that may have been written in Egypt between 3,000 and 1,000 BCE and contained vastly superior medical and philosophical knowledge. This knowledge was destroyed as civilisation headed towards the arrival of the one-god religious dynasties after 01 AD Hermes became merely a winged messenger god who could pass between the Underworld and the Upperworld, often escorting souls. He can be seen in the illustration at the beginning of this chapter. Even in this watered down version, he still sends a clear message that wisdom and knowledge will help us mortals in our dealings with the Underworld.

In ancient Egypt magic and healing were taken to be the same thing. The supernatural were called on by chanting invocations whilst treating the patient. This would have invoked the secret power of the unconscious, which is what is also invoked during the healing ceremony of reiki. This is often called the placebo effect by medical science.

This is a quote from a book on the website of Professor Ralph Abraham (Princeton, Berkeley and California Universities):

"With these spells, evolved over centuries, one might... communicate with the gods, command subtle energies, acquire wealth and health. The most powerful allies were the gods and goddesses of the underworld, Erishkegal, Persephone, Hekate and the like. We are left with the impression that magic is a human creation which exists on a level above religion. While religions come and go, magic is eternal."[23]

While Scorpio is indeed associated with the mastery of healing, there are two sides to the coin, and I will just remind you about the myth involving Asclepius, who is the Greek god of medicine whom the medical profession these days *do* want to be associated with. (His is the rod with the single serpent on it.) Asclepius was curing so many people and even bringing them back from the dead, that Pluto feared he would have no more souls left in the Underworld, so he asked Zeus to kill Asclepius. He was duly wiped out with a thunderbolt, and became a constellation in the sky. The interesting point here is that Pluto *must* maintain the amount of souls on the journey. This process must continue above all efforts to preserve life here on earth. So the medical profession had better watch out. If they keep too many of us alive they'll all get the old thunderbolt treatment! What Pluto gives, he can also remove.

Interestingly, a doctor today swears a Hippocratic oath when he qualifies. Hippocrates used astrology and his medicine was based on the movement of the heavens. He would not advocate surgery when the Moon was in the Zodiac sign connected to that part of the body, and he warned of the rising of certain stars such as Sirius.

The difference between dark feminine and dark masculine

If Tiamat is an expression of the extreme dark face of feminine, then what is the extreme dark face of masculine? To answer this question we have to first recognise that the dark face of feminine is about extreme *feelings*. So the opposite, dark masculine, has to be about an extreme *lack* of feelings, and this then is psychopathy. A human being is psychopathic when he or she is devoid of feeling. An extreme example of this could be found in Germany during the Second World War, where a dream of perfection was turned into a destructive force. In this way 'destroying' occurs in both dark feminine and dark masculine. Dark masculine is the 'hero' on the hero's journey taken to extreme, the zealous militant with ideals of perfectionism and a Utopian vision.

Imagine for a moment a circle. As the astrolological number for Pluto is zero or nought, then this seems quite fitting. This circle is the circle of life, and everything in life goes round in a continuous loop. Now imagine two 'poles' like the north and south poles of our planet. Masculine and feminine are polar opposites, with one at the top and one at the bottom, but they blend into each other at the Equator, where things could be considered balanced. In this way, masculine emerges out of feminine and then feminine emerges out of masculine. As with the chicken and the egg, I don't think we'll ever know which came first! Being at the extreme 'pole' of either is ugly, but of the two options feminine can seem the most attractive when we ask the question "Who wants to be cured of feelings and desire?"

Pluto represents feminine energy despite the fact that the name Pluto comes from a male Greek god. Pluto experiences speak eloquently of the rage, fury and wrath inherent in feminine energy. There can be power struggles and jealousy within relationships or when children are born, which are quite common during the times that we are personally receiving energy from Pluto. Feelings of protective primal savagery can tap us on the shoulder when we are creating something that stirs us deeply and we want to protect it at all costs.

What we can expect to gain, change and develop in the 21st Century?

We shall find parallel universes, the Underworld and Heaven of Mythology

According to top physicist Professor Max Tegmark, "The key question is not whether parallel universes exist but how many levels there are."[24]

Because Pluto represents hidden realms and dimensions we can expect quantum leaps of discovery in this area. We could never have imagined in the 1980s that scientists would be using words like 'ether', when discussing particles that pop in and out of our dimension. The spiritual and mythological claims that dark, unseen dimensions existed were ridiculed by many mainstream academics. Now we get such eminent scientists as Brian Greene telling us that:

> "The entire Universe is this gigantic loaf with many other
> slices, potentially. So our Universe could be one slice, and a
> different parallel universe could be living on a different slice."[25]

This book seeks to establish the probability that these parallel universes include the Underworld or Duat of the very ancient civilisations, and also the heaven of more recent religions. The Christian image of Hell is more likely to be this world, the 4 per cent, since it contains so much atrocity.

Scientific exploration is proceeding at breathtaking speed and many textbooks are out of date before they are printed. Such is this pace that we will no doubt have as much inter-dimensional experience as we can manage to understand before the 21st century has ended. As this unfolds, there is an amazing similarity between the descriptions and words of the spiritual texts left us from many thousands of years ago, and the scientific discoveries of today. The two seem to be converging into a common knowledge, which is interesting, since neither party wants to be identified with a view that they had previously considered un-enlightened. It is, however, very gratifying for those of us who have upheld spiritual knowledge for all these years.

The changes to Pluto coincide with the development of the Large Hadron Collider

As I write this, we are witnessing the launch of the most ambitious experiment that science has ever taken on. The Large Hadron Collider has a mission to discover tiny, invisible particles of energy that will inform us of parallel universes and other dimensions. The whole project was synchronous with Pluto from the beginning and it is interesting to look at what has been happening to Pluto the planet, with reference to the progress of the project.

I wrote a little about the LHC in chapter two, but I will say more about it now.

The scientists involved in the project are trying to find out what matter is made of. We know that it is made of cells, and cells are made of molecules, and molecules are made of atoms and atoms are made of smaller elements called particles. But when they look into these particles they find a lot of spinning energy and what looks like empty space. *Something* has to provide atoms with weight/mass/substance, but where is it? The theory is that there are *invisible* undetectable 'dark' particles and 'dark' matter which, if accounted for, will explain how an atom is rigid. These dark particles probably exist in a fourth dimension that intertwines with ours and the LHC has been constructed to find this other dimension.

To find the dark particles, beams of energy with particles of 'real' matter in them are sent whirling round inside an underground circular tube at the speed of light. Then another one is sent in the opposite direction. Periodically these collide, and large detectors measure the invisible energy that is released. Measuring this released energy tells them about the dark particles in the other dimension.

One of the most obvious symbols of relationship between Pluto and the LHC is the shape. It is a 27 kilometres long tunnel formed into a circle, and the beams it produces go round inside it. Not only is this the shape of the number zero, which is the sacred number of Pluto, the circle is also the symbol of the cycle of life. Another obvious synchronicity is the LHC's physical position, buried deep within the bowels of the Earth – a real underworld!

In 1995 Pluto moved into the ninth Zodiac sign, Sagittarius, which is the part of the sky most associated with the search for the truth and spiritual meaning of life. When Pluto moves through any Zodiac sign it is expected that worldwide events will focus on the meanings of that sign, and certainly the quest and journey that sub-atomic physics has been on has been very descriptive of Sagittarius, with huge leaps into wild, unbridled theories and breakthroughs. The European consortium that built the LHC reported that their energy capacity for sub-atomic research doubled in the year that Pluto moved into Sagittarius "opening up important new discovery domains."[26] Sagittarius describes higher spiritual learning, and the seeking of the vision of the Divine. During the years that Pluto was in this sign, from 1995 to 2008, the LHC was being built with a vision of the possibility of finding the origins of life.

In 2006 things began to get really exciting. Pluto lined up between the Earth and the centre of our Galaxy, which is in the last few degrees of Sagittarius. This point is known in astrology to be immensely powerful. There is actually a large black hole there, and it had the effect of plugging Pluto energy into the national grid. All the digging and building work at the LHC ended and they started installing and operating the very high voltage machines that would enable their sub-atomic research. For the next two years, all sorts of experimental achievements were accomplished. Then, as Pluto stood for the last few days close to the galactic center, the first beams of energy were officially sent all the way around the ring at the LHC for the first time and the machine started up. The timing of the two events was co-incidental, and as if to confirm the astrological importance, our Moon also joined Pluto there for a few hours. Her quiet and reflective light provided the calm before the storm of worldwide media attention the next day.

The press coverage before the inauguration invoked the usual responses that Pluto tends to generate. Some embraced the future possibilities with excitement, some ignored them for now, and others become fearful of catastrophe and tried to prevent it all happening with legal challenges. It was interesting to see that the PR people in charge began selling the project with the line that they were attempting to re-create the moment after the Big Bang. This might be true enough, but it glossed over the fact that they were looking for evidence of energy reappearing and disappearing into other dimensions. The 'other dimensions' talk had frightened the press and public into thinking that the Earth was going to disappear into a black hole, so this aspect of the research became underplayed.

The Zodiac sign after Sagittarius is Capricorn, and Pluto moved fully into this earth sign in November 2008. Since the LHC intends to smash ions of lead together, it seems amazing that this should happen just at the time that Pluto moves into the Zodiac sign most associated with lead and dense matter. Capricorn is the highest initiation of matter and the earth element, and is ruled by Saturn, the planet that ruled the outer limits of our known world for thousands of years. Those 'outer limits' are a frontier that will be well and truly smashed in the 21st century!

The development and acceptance of atomic energy

The term 'nuclear' comes from the 'nucleus' of an atom, and in an atom there is a force so strong it can be turned into a bomb that can destroy a whole city. There are understandably deeply rooted public concerns about nuclear power. Many of those alive today can remember the fear invoked by the use of the atom bomb during the 20th century. Add to that the incidents such as the Chernobyl disaster, and it is understandable why the public are so against it. Concerns range from the disposal of the radioactive waste product, to the easy production of nuclear weapons. But nuclear bombs were built before anybody thought of using it to produce electricity. When they built and used the bombs in 1945 there were no nuclear reactors in existence. Proof that countries can build bombs without nuclear power stations.

The nuclear industry is now keen to point out that if nuclear power stations are properly managed then they are an environmentally safe, pollution-free source of electricity. According to the chairman of the International Atomic Energy Agency in 2004, "in contrast with the 25 *billion* tonnes of carbon waste released directly into the atmosphere every year from fossil fuels, the amount of nuclear waste seems relatively small."[27]

I suspect that governments will be forced to re-think their current opposition towards building any more nuclear power stations, because fossil fuels will not be available for much longer. New options should open up with regard to nuclear power however, with maybe a whole new way of using the latent power trapped in the nucleus of an atom. Invisible forces of nature may become known and available to us.

Can we change our perception of evil and the Devil?

Unfortunately, a few Dennis Wheatley films, and 2,000 years of being told that terror and damnation awaits us in an Underworld of burning hellfire and purgatory have left us feeling very fearful. This fear stops us from feeling comfortable about an investigation into the contents of Pluto's box. The words Hades and death have become synonymous with evil. But the Underworld is not filled with evil or horned goblins with toasting forks, and I think our society will now finally emerge from the shadow of the Middle Ages. There *is* another dimension or parallel universe, and science has now proven that, but it supports our Universe and we should not fear it.

Really evil acts of a barbaric and psychotic nature do happen. This is undeniable, but these happen because of mental illness, fear, ignorance, or the primordial, brutal, animalistic instincts that remain hard-wired into our human nature. This instinct is a relic of some savage and prehistoric past, when we had to go out to club the beast. It was necessary then to take a knife to the throat of a living animal, but evolution has, by and large, removed the need for most of us to do this. However, the ability to kill still remains deeply embedded in our genetic inheritance, should we ever find ourselves in need of it again in future centuries. Having that potential on the hard drive of human DNA is protective of the human race should the flood or the apocalypse ever happen again. It means that the survival of the fittest will ensure that strong and robust parents give birth to strong and robust children. The human race will survive and flourish again. This is the underlying code of universal natural law, which will maintain the procreation and survival of the human race at any cost to the individual. This is what Pluto really represents. Pluto doesn't have to be barbaric. This energy is not naturally destructive for the sake of it. It has a purpose.

The image of Pluto, Hades and the Underworld is one that we are trying to avoid in our technically advanced society. Many scientists scoff at the idea of God or the Devil and believe that they can confine Pluto to a petri-dish, remove the undesirable and control the outcome.

The more spiritually inclined of us flinch from 'dark' issues like Satan and death, preferring to talk of pink, fluffy angels. It is hard to accept and deal with the destructive, dark and painful forces that threaten disintegration of cherished ideals. But by refusing to know the dark side, we move away from the possibility of a deep and real understanding of it. Perhaps we are throwing the baby out with the bath water. We actually need to gain a *deeper* knowledge and mastery of the unconscious, and the fundamental forces of our life here on earth. As far as astrology and science is concerned, each and every one of us has a dark side, but it's how much fear, ignorance and impotence controls us that regulates its effects on our lives. The more we understand something, the greater our intelligence and the more we are empowered. We have more options or choice, because we can consider more. Modern psychology believes that anything we fear and push into our unconscious simply gathers more energy and re-routes. It may then pop up as energy that we constellate or magnetise into our lives. It may appear as if it is entirely another person's doing, but it will appear. And then we are *really* ill equipped to deal with it.

One of the things that Scorpio is traditionally known for is the 'occult'. This word always conjures up thoughts of witchcraft and evil, but let's look at what it means. The definition of occult in my dictionary is:

"Involving mystical or supernatural phenomena or powers. Beyond ordinary human understanding. Secret or mysterious."

Supernatural is "something that cannot be explained by science." So the word occult by itself is not that scary. Satan is a fear in our minds.

The changing of Pluto's official status from planet to binary planetoid system has symbolised an immense and imminent universal change. Perhaps now we can seek to understand the emerging power, with all the taboo issues and fearfulness that this brings. We might want to understand for our spiritual peace of mind, but also so we can work with this omnipresent cosmic force, perhaps see the beauty, elegance and magnificence, and at least become respectful of the immense power it wields. It is likely that healing and growth can be found through the mastery and understanding that a thorough examination of the Underworld can bring.

Let's look at the meaning of the word 'Pluto'. It comes from the Greek word 'plouton' meaning wealth. Another definition is 'rich'. I truly believe there are riches to be gained from Pluto's world, if we accept a rough ride with trust and faith in a higher divine power.

Understanding the meaning of life can change our attitude to death and the afterlife

I wrote briefly in chapter three about how we might change our attitude to death, but I would like to just touch on it again. Since fear is usually brought about by not knowing, the 'knowing' that we are likely to get in the near future should alleviate the terrible fear that death invokes in us. Loss will still occur as loved ones pass on into the 96 per cent and mourning for the loss of the loved one is an essential part of being human, but a much deeper understanding of *why* it has to happen is now available. Knowing the meaning of life, and the part our soul plays in it, answers questions that our curiosity has yearned for centuries. At last, that information is here for us to gain.

Basically, there is a Multiverse of many universes. Life as we know it occurs in just one Universe, and this is everything we know, the planets, stars and Earth. This is just 4 per cent of the Multiverse. The dark or missing 96 per cent is the rest of the Multiverse and it includes an Underworld that our soul goes to when we die. Our deceased soul empties out its life experiences and wisdom into the Collective ocean or great soup of Collective Soul. And our soul's contribution improves the overall wisdom and experience of this Collective Soul. Our soul is then recycled into the next appropriate 'life' cycle. This might be back to the Earthly plane in the 4 per cent, or on to higher transcendence.

The human race has to survive at all costs, because this is the Multiverse's only solid expression of the energy and intelligence that exists in the chaos and timelessness of the 96 per cent.

If you just followed that, you may not need the rest of this book!

Much of that is not new. We have been told it by our ancient texts. What is new is that the Underworld is one of these other parallel universes or dimensions.

Miraculous healing potential, reiki and Kundalini

Numerous web sites equate the power of the serpent with Kundalini reiki. In *'Myths and Gods of India'* we are told that Siva carries a snake around his neck and phallus, and:

> "...the main meaning attached to the serpent is to represent the basic dormant energy, akin to the sexual power, which is coiled at the base of the spinal cord, and supports attempts to conquer higher worlds during inward journeys. This energy, source of

all spiritual conquests, is called Kundalini, the coiled serpent power."[28]

According to a professional American medical website:

"An occult description of the staff with two snakes winding up it is that the serpents may represent positive and negative Kundalini as it moves through the chakras and around the spine (the staff) to the head where it communicates with mind..."[29]

Kundalini contains the potential for spiritual transformation and is often activated by major life events such as a near death experience or the birth of a child. While this might sound frightening, it should be stressed that Kundalini is the Hindu word for sacred, transformative, awakening energy, and surely this is sought by anyone who seeks spiritual enlightenment. It seems that powerful life events have the potential to take us into higher states of consciousness, and this is whether they are willingly sought in a peaceful meditative way, or whether they come with tragedy and loss. Either way, Pluto's generative abilities are being accessed in these periods of immense change and transformation, and that's an awful lot of nuclear power to have at your disposal! It is during these periods that the 'wealth' of Pluto is available on a soul level.

'*Myths of India*' infers that the same Kundalini energy is available in a universal, macro form when it gives birth to the Universe, and in a personal, micro form when it can lead to awakening and liberation. As astrology is telling us that Pluto is going to become much more accessible and understandable in the forthcoming years, then the implication is that we will all be able to access much greater personal awakening, including that of our individual latent healing potential. Medical science is already recording the effects of this.

New Scientist reported in late 2008 that "the placebo effect appears to be growing stronger in clinical trials, causing problems for drug companies attempting to prove their products are better than placebo."[30]

This is evidence of the growing power of the human consciousness to access the power of the deep realms, and bring about miraculous healing. This is exceptionally good news for reiki, which taps into deep personal and universal realms for its Pluto-nic energy.

Just one more thing whilst we are on the subject of healing. Take a moment to think about what is required to get rid of a pimple or boil. It needs to be destroyed and the poison removed before the healing can begin. Pluto is the energy that will bring about the end of something. Without it the boil would just go on forever!

Transformation, evolution and 'wealth' on a soul level

When a client comes to me asking for information about when they can extricate themselves from a bad marriage, or an unsuitable job, the first thing I look for are the dates when Pluto will be influencing them, and those are the dates they get! With the right advice they can channel, bend and transpose the incoming energy at that time to get the changes they dream of, although they must be prepared to accept a lot of change, some of which may include loss. In astrology, Pluto represents a powerful energy that will challenge or assist our journey to higher consciousness, although it has always been the most feared.

However, we are told in the myths of Persephone and Inanna, that we *will* come out of the Underworld again, and we will have gained much wealth and riches during our time in the depths. It is now time to accept transformation, evolution and wealth with good grace!

5

CHARON, GUIDE TO PLUTO AND THE INVISIBLE REALMS

7 *A mortal getting into Charon's boat, watched over by Hermes*

Charon, a partner for Pluto

Now here's a planet you won't have heard of! For many years Pluto was thought to be the last and furthest planet from the Sun. We have never sent a spacecraft or probe there, and all we have are some hazy images of a distant blob of light. Recently, space instruments and telescopes have become much more sophisticated and we have started to learn a lot more. Surprisingly, we found out that Pluto has a partner planet called Charon, *and* there are an additional two moons in orbit around them. There seems to be a close relationship between our discoveries about Pluto and the those of the particles in an atom. There is more to an atom than previously thought, and Pluto's neighbourhood in space is also filled with hitherto unknown bodies. Discoveries in one area of our world are always synchronous with discoveries in another.

How Charon was discovered

Back in 1978 a US Navy astronomer was doing some precise observations of Pluto due to the fact that it had moved closer to the Sun than normal. In fact Pluto had even moved *inside* the orbit of next planet, which happens for only 20 years of its 248 year cycle around the Sun. Astronomer James Christy noticed that some of the photographs of Pluto appeared to show a bulge of light at the side of the planet, and after much checking it was officially announced to the world that this bulge was actually a separate 'moon' and it was given the name Charon. Soon after discovery, Charon and Pluto obligingly posed for photographs. The timing was amazing as the pair wouldn't be in the same position again for centuries.[1]

The discoverer named Charon after the ferryman of Greek mythology, who takes the souls of the dead across a river into the Underworld. He asked that Charon be pronounced *Shar-on*, after his wife Charlene.[2]

Because astronomers can only estimate the size of such far off bodies by measuring the amount of light they reflect, the discovery of Charon changed all previous perceptions about the size of Pluto. Now that the light given off it had to be divided by two, it meant that that Pluto was not as bright, and therefore not as big. As our perception of Pluto was divided into smaller pieces, so was our perception of the atom.

Pluto and Charon are locked into each other in the same way that the two ends of a dumbbell are attached. It's as if an invisible shaft holds them together. They are so close, the centre of gravity for each planet is not within itself, but in the space between the two planets, and their two faces are permanently frozen together.

As the 21st century dawned astronomers were setting up equipment for the survey that would discover what was in the Kuiper Belt, which is the region around Pluto and Charon. The new planets they discovered are in the chapters following this, but we just need to look at one thing about that survey that had big impact on Pluto and Charon.

Because the survey discovered more planets after Pluto-Charon and they didn't want to keep re-writing the textbooks, they had to come up with a different definition of the term 'planet'. The new definition meant that Charon qualified for the new term 'dwarf planet' and in 2006 this was announced.[3] A big step up for Charon. However, that same announcement demoted Pluto from a planet to a dwarf planet. This made them a very unusual double dwarf planet or 'binary' planet, and there is a lot of spiritual meaning that can be inferred by this, as we shall see later.

Charon struggling to be accepted

Even though all the above happened as stated, Charon's designation as dwarf planet has not found acceptance with some astronomers. The other dwarf planets are heavily promoted by their extrovert and enthusiastic discoverer, Mike Brown, but it seems that Charon's half-life in the shadow of Pluto is going to be hard to shake off. However, there will be more interest in future years when a space probe arrives at Pluto-Charon in 2015. This mission was launched by NASA in January 2006 and is called New Horizons.

The mythological world of ancient Greece and how this might represent the Multiverse

On 15th May 2005, two small moons were discovered around Pluto-Charon. They were called Nix and Hydra, so the whole Pluto-Charon family has been given mythological names from the ancient Greek

Underworld. Before we go on to look at what that might mean, it is useful to see how the ancient Greeks viewed the Multiverse.

The three 'realms' in their myths consisted of the Upperworld of mortal humans, the Underworld where the souls or shades of the dead mortals go, and Olympus which was the home of Zeus and his family. It was high up a mountain and protected by a gate shrouded in clouds.[4] Other deities might reside in the earth or water of the Upperworld, but they could visit Olympus for pleasure.

The 'Heavens', were a celestial backdrop to Olympus, a stage which they could play things out on if they wished.[5] A god could be banished to the stars where he would become a constellation, and that's where he stayed. While Olympus itself was a separate place, the gods and goddesses could mingle with the mortals on Earth, (Upperworld) and their lives were intertwined with ours, often invisibly so. The Underworld could be reached from the Upperworld or from the Heavens.

Are these two mythological places metaphors for the dimensions that the scientists will now discover? We will find dimensions that exist alongside and intertwined with ours. Maybe we can interpret one as the Underworld, a repository or great lake of soul energy in which our souls are recycled, and maybe there is another which is like Olympus, full of spirit, energy, and represents the God-ness and the spiritual element of fire.

The myths of Charon, Nix and Hydra from the Underworld

Charon is the ancient Greek name given to a mythical ferryman who takes the souls of the dead across a river into the Underworld. *Bulfinch's Mythology* says:

> "They then came to black river, where they found the ferryman,
> Charon, old and squalid, but strong and vigorous, who was
> receiving passengers of all kinds into his boat… they stood
> pressing for a passage and longing to touch the opposite shore.

But the stern ferryman took in only such as he chose, driving the rest back. Those who are taken on board the bark are the souls of those who have received due burial rites; the host of others who have remained unburied are not permitted to pass the flood, but wander a hundred years… until at last they are taken over (the river)."[6]

The story then relates how two living people were permitted to travel across the river because they carried a golden branch, a symbol that Charon recognises. There are at least four mythical instances of the living going into the Underworld and getting out again, so clearly it *can* be done, although all the myths initially give it a 'land-of-no-return' image. Those that do praise the process for the riches it gives. Elsewhere we learn that Charon expects coins in payment for his ferrying of the souls of the dead. In the past, a coin used to be placed under the tongue of the deceased.[7] Another tale tells us that as the souls stand on the bank waiting to be ferried by Charon, they resemble birds as they gather together to seek warmer climes at the first chill of winter, or leaves, waiting to fall from the branches in autumn.[8]

In myth, Charon is a member of a very gloomy family, which reinforces the dark underworld theme of the whole clan. His mother is a Greek deity called Nyx, and a derivation of this name was given to one of the two Pluto-Charon Moons found in 2006, so we kill two birds with one stone if we look at the origins surrounding that mythological family. In a nutshell, the whole clan is about the creation. Charon's grandmother is Chaos, the original nothingness, which was there before there was anything else. Therefore she is the quantum energy of pre-existence, what was there in the beginning, before the Big Bang.

Chaos created Erebos, who is called primordial darkness or the darkness of the Underworld,[9] and his sister, Nyx, who is the goddess of the night or the darkness of the Earth. They gave birth to many children, called Doom of Death, Fate of Death, Sleep, Dreams, Criticism, Deceit,

Sex, Old Age, and Strife, to name but a few. However, she also gave birth to Ether, Day and Air, symbolising the equal power of light and dark. It is said that she also gave birth to Eros, god of desire, who was known for shooting arrows at people to make them fall in lust.

Although Nyx was rarely mentioned in Greek myth, her power was emphasised when it was said that Zeus backed away from her in one encounter, an unimaginable event, considering he was the King of the Gods with a temper and an ego to match. She was sometimes represented as a veil of dark mist, drawn forth from the Underworld, which blotted out the light.[10]

The last myth we have to look at is that of Hydra, the other moon that was discovered in 2006. Hydra was a serpent or water snake of Greek mythology that lived in a marsh near the mouth of the Underworld and had nine heads. If a head was severed, two grew back. Hercules was sent to kill this monster as the second of his 12 labours. He used fire to cauterise the wound of each head as it fell off so that none could grow again. This might represent one of those problems that seems to get bigger as you attack it, and so might need a constantly positive belief in the power of spirit. After killing the beast, Hercules dipped two arrows in the poisonous blood. These arrows caused him to harm two friends, and eventually brought about his own death. Perhaps the moral of the story is after the fight and the victory, don't take any of the venom with you. It will have dire consequences if you do!

The spiritual meaning of Charon

The importance of the ferryman in significant ancient texts

The ancient texts of the Egyptians and the Mesopotamians (the first master race who lived in Iraq) also have ferrymen. The pyramid texts of ancient Egypt, written around 3,000 BCE say *"Hdhd*, the ferryman of the Winding Watercourse, comes…".[11] Hundreds of miles away and about 1,000 years later, the Mesopotamian myth called the 'Epic of

Gilgamesh', written in approx. 2,000 BCE advises us that a boatman crosses the waters of Death.[12]

So the idea of a ferryman remained in the Middle East for thousands of years. It's a simple idea, but it begs the question of why Charon has suddenly become important to astrology, and why is that important to the human race now? Why do we need a ferryman again?

A symbol of the beginning of an immense and epic journey of discovery for the human race

If you've made it this far, dear reader, then you are about to find out why I am making such a big deal out of this whole Charon thing!

The ancients knew that immense journeys of discovery required a spiritual guide. We are being told that we are going on a journey of discovery, and something or someone is going to guide us through this potentially difficult passage. Charon the ferryman was not just the tour guide, he decided who got on the bus and whether or not they were spiritually prepared enough to board.

As a planet, he managed to hide his existence from us until such time as we were ready. It's as if the planet (or godness) is saying "OK, you have the technology to discover my presence. This technology will now take you on a journey, and I am your stern guide and overseer."

OK, so what's the journey?

Well, it could be the discovery of the other dimensions I have talked about. If we use our Solar System as an analogy, then the Pluto-Charon family represents the Underworld, and that is within the larger Kuiper Belt, which in general represents the other dimensions of the Multiverse. Pluto-Charon is like a sentry or gateway into the Kuiper Belt. Of course, there *are* other ways into the Kuiper Belt. We could send a rocket from Earth in any direction and it will get there eventually, since the Kuiper Belt surrounds us. But Pluto-Charon was the first known bit of it, and that's where we are sending a space probe. So the metaphor is saying we have to enter the Underworld, or cross over from our dimension into the Underworld in order to access the dimensions from whence we came. We were told this by the ancient Egyptians. Charon is the ferryman who stands at the gateway, just as he does in the myth. He will allow us passage if we are properly prepared, but not before.

Another journey might be our quest to discover our origins, which is similar of course. The Greek myth of creation actually says that in the beginning was Chaos and this gave birth to Night, Darkness and Day etc. and the human race is currently discovering the science of that creation, about our formation out of pure energy and chaotic quantum-ruled atoms. How we emerged from the energy of pre-existence into the world of matter and form that we know. The 'fall' of Man, or the Big Bang, is when our Universe fell out of the quantum chaos of the primordial soup into the order of the Upperworld.[13]

What does Duality mean?

NASA says, "Pluto has a dual identity."[14] The dwarf planets, Pluto and Charon, are locked into each other as if an invisible shaft joins them. We are being asked to understand that the most powerful force in astrology is now two, not one. That Pluto has another face, and that there is another side to this energy.

Duality was highly prized by the Ancient Egyptians, and they used the serpent to symbolise it. So what is duality and why is it important?

Well, to start with, the dictionary says that duality means having two parts, functions or aspects. This might be useful because we don't know what anything is, until we can see the difference. If we live in perpetual light, how do we know what dark is? Only after it has turned dark do we notice the difference and ask, "What was it that has gone missing? What is this that I am in now?"

The ability to think about the meaning of opposites gives a framework in which we can use free will to organise and balance our lives. If you can see that this is white, but you want to be more black, you can use absolute black and absolute white as your outer markers, and aim for darker or lighter grey, depending on your choice. Having duality, or two parts, functions or aspects to choose from or measure by, is giving us choice.

Then we discriminate, we think this way, then that way. We analyse and develop intelligence and intuition along the way. We create opportunity and then we destroy it when it is past its 'sell by' date. We use the energy of Pluto to build and dismantle.

And why is that important?

There are millions of souls on a spiral journey of evolution, and they must all contribute to a rising of the universal Collective 'mind' into higher consciousness. Our separate pieces of knowledge and understanding are gathered together to move the whole of life onto higher planes of awareness. Things like choices and dual importance create the friction and tension that make us work at balance and greater awareness and wisdom. We improve and refine ourselves as we work to explore the different options that are in front of us. The coins we have to pay the ferryman in the myth are the pearls of wisdom we have gained in our lives. Remember in the myth if we don't have enough coins to pay the ferryman, we are left to wander the banks of the river for a time? The more often we grow and evolve through the crisis and change which Pluto's world invokes, the more often we benefit by having the right amount of coins. In Greek, the word Pluto comes from the word *plouton*, which means wealth or riches.

For 40 years very little was discovered in our Solar System. Then we went through a period of accelerated discovery starting in 2003. It means the human race is leaping forward in spiritual understanding too. However, the ferryman clearly thinks the time has come for us to understand the Underworld, which we are told holds wealth and richness. The payoffs will be a source of atomic power that is safe for our planet, scientific understanding of other dimensions and other universes in the Multiverse and an understanding of our creation.

The ferryman has come to show us the real truth about the Underworld. Charon is guiding us on a whole new journey.

6

MAKEMAKE, THE GREAT SEA SPIRIT OF EASTER ISLAND

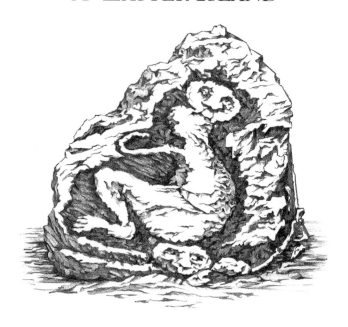

8 *An image of Makemake carved on a rock on Easter Island*

Our journey now leaves the ancient Greek Underworld and we travel many thousands of miles to the Pacific Ocean. Here we visit two Polynesian islands. The first, Easter Island, the home of Makemake and then Hawaii, the home of Haumea, both new energies or deities that will walk with us during the frantic changes of the 21st century. Since they have only recently re-emerged, it will take us some time to understand what they mean in depth, but this chapter is a start. Well, quite a big start actually! It is the largest chapter in this book, but this is no reflection of Makemake's strength or prominence over the rest of the dwarf planets, since there are others that feel stronger. It is simply that there is so much that we weren't aware of before. Prepare for an amazing tale if you have not yet heard the history of Easter Island.

Makemake, the dwarf planet

One of the greatest difficulties this dwarf planet may have in gaining public affection is the fact that the name is difficult to pronounce. If you can say something without feeling dumb or disrespectful it has more endearing qualities! However, I suspect when you have finished this chapter you will look again at that name, and see it differently.

Makemake is one of four newly discovered dwarf planets in the region called the Kuiper Belt, and is entirely new to astrology, and our spiritual awareness. He was the god of a little known people who had suffered a great tragedy, but they also had powerful spiritual beliefs that came closer to the 'reality' of our existence than anything the western world was thinking at the time.

Knowing about the energy of Makemake brings a spiritual acceptance that embraces and opens our unconsciousness to living with him. He represents an important branch of existence that we need to understand so can we accept and harmonise with what the Divine wants from us. So despite Makemake's distance from us, both as a planet and as the spiritual deity of a very distant homeland, we need to pay him homage, reverence and thoughtfulness. To do this we need to learn more about him.

How Makemake was given his unusual name

Makemake the planet was discovered on March 31st 2005 by a team of three astronomers, Mike Brown, Chad Trujillo and David Rabinowitz. Because it was Easter, they initially gave it the nickname of Easterbunny, which they kept for the next three years because they couldn't think of anything else! The team wanted to choose names from religions and mythology outside of the usual ancient Greek and Roman choices, breaking with centuries of tradition. Mike was very careful and thoughtful in his choice of names, and we should be extremely grateful for that, because it has given us instant spiritual understanding. However, the inspiration to name this new planet was slow in coming. Because of the Easter connection, he had considered the pagan goddess Eostre, but then found that an asteroid already had that name. He considered rabbit gods, including one called Manabozho, but said that none seemed right and so he left it for another year. Recognising that the project was soon to end and the public were loosing interest, the IAU threatened to name the dwarf planet themselves, forcing Mike to make a decision in 2008. He had a flash of inspiration and remembered the name of Easter Island in the South Pacific, discovered on Easter Sunday in 1722. This gave the island and the planet the same birthday, 283 years apart. He searched mythology for the name of a god while remembering how masculine fertility and fecundity had overwhelmed him at the time of the discovery because he was going to become a father for the first time.[1] Mike said that what he read about Makemake felt absolutely right to him, confirming that this deity and planet were really communicating with him.

The story of Easter Island

There had to be a reason why the Divine chose, through astrology, to make this forgotten little island important, and I was curious as I ordered a pile of science journals and books, thinking, "Astrology's gone a bit weird here. There can't be anything of interest on a volcano in the middle of the Pacific Ocean…" I started reading the first book, and after the first three chapters I unplugged the phone and told my daughter to get takeaways for a month or two. This is a very tragic story, which I decided to tell in full to honour the people. I can only hope the decision to name a planet after this poor little island's chief god will improve its lot in life and perhaps Makemake hopes this too.

Easter Island has the most isolated position in the world. It is about 2,400 miles to the nearest significant land, Chile, and it takes five to six hours to get there by air. On the map below, the dot in the middle of the circle is Easter Island, in the ocean in between Chile and Polynesia.

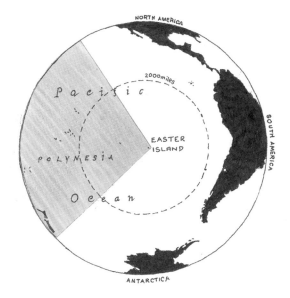

9 *The dot in the middle of the circle is Easter Island. The dotted circle shows the emptiness of the 2,000 miles around the island. The shaded area on the left is the extent of Polynesia, a vast ocean containing a few small islands*

(Adapted. See refs.)

Polynesia is actually not a country, but a vast ocean, with a few islands in it. Two thousand years ago people travelled great distances across the sea as easily as we do now, but without modern navigational aids. How Easter Island got populated is hotly debated by academics. There is evidence that explorers arrived on Easter Island from both the Americas and Polynesia in the first millennium, which would make sense, since the island is in the middle of the two cultures. And although the Polynesians have certainly been the most obvious with the American influence being relatively weak, the collision and fusion of these two great peoples has made Easter Island a very special place with history, customs and beliefs that cannot be found anywhere else.

The island itself is only 13 miles by 11 miles by 10 miles, and shaped like a triangle. It has a mild climate with an average temperature of 20°C, albeit a tad windy. Each tip of the triangle is a volcano which rises up 10,000 feet from the seabed. They huddle together in a group like a triple-peaked mountain, except that the peaks are volcanic craters filled with reeds and stagnant water. There is fertile grass growing on the plains and slopes in between these peaks. The island sits on a fault line that goes all the way back to the Andes Mountains in South America (important because of the Nazca lines). This crack in the Earth's crust actually branches under Easter Island, which makes it a 'hot spot'. There is so much molten lava coming to the surface of the Earth here, that the island could either erupt or sink at any time and in fact there was a lava flow about 2,500 years ago.[2] Whole islands can suddenly appear or disappear in this area and myth has a god who levers them up and down.

Since 1888 the island has been part of Chile, with a population of circa 4,000 in 2004, and is heavily dependent on Chilean subsidies. However, the island was colonised by a good number of Polynesians and confusingly its people and language are called 'Rapanui', while the island is locally known as Rapa Nui.

In the late 19th century a holocaust brought about by Europeans and Peruvians nearly wiped out the entire population, along with much of the indigenous spiritual knowledge, the structure and hierarchy of their culture and ancient artefacts. This is described fully later.

These days, Easter Island is known mostly for what *couldn't* be destroyed and this has become one of the biggest unsolved mysteries of our time. The island is covered with hundreds of giant stone statues called mo'ai, that were made to stand on equally giant stone built platforms around the coast. These statues weigh up to 270 tons each and would have presented as great a challenge to the Islanders as the pyramids did to the Egyptians. Just as big a mystery is why they suddenly stopped producing them. Some were still being carved when one day the workers put down their tools and never went back! Another unsolved mystery is the strange hieroglyphic writing found here that appears nowhere else in the world. The royalty and priesthood who understood it were all killed, and missionaries destroyed most of it. Just a few pieces of it remain to this day. The Polynesians never developed a writing system so where did it come from?

Other unusual features of the island are ancient rock carvings and the caves the Islanders used to live in at times. These were air bubbles that formed in the cooling lava of the volcano, and the island is riddled with them. Swedish anthropologist Thor Heyerdahl commented that "Easter Island is a world on two levels."[3] When he lived there in the 1950s there was a daylight world of reed huts and Christianity on the surface, with a world of ancient charms, superstitions, sorcery and mystery played out in secret caves at night. The Islanders knew two realities.

The island's different names

It seems that one of the many injustices has been the name we call the island. The earliest Islanders called it 'Te Pito te Henua' which meant centre or navel of the world. The South American Inca capital also had a name that meant 'navel of the Earth' so there is obviously some sort of connection between the two.[4] The Islanders liked the name because their volcano with a deep lagoon in it reminded them of a navel.

French officials returning sick kidnapped Islanders in the mid 1860s made a confused association with another island, and ended up calling it Rapa Nui, the official Polynesian name it has today. However, the Spanish call it Isla de Pascua, and the English use the more affectionate name of Easter Island, which is the name I shall use.

History of the Easter Islanders

The outstanding seamanship and astronomy of the ancient Polynesians

Our journey towards understanding this deeply spiritual, brave and sensitive race begins with their seamanship and star reading skills. Advance scouts would leave Polynesian islands in ocean-going double-hulled canoes and travel thousands of miles to seek new lands. Then they would go back and advise the others, who would then emigrate. Scientists have dismissed this simply on the grounds that these were un-evolved primitives who had no technological instruments. Hmm, let's ponder on that point. Why do we insist that races that precede us could not have accomplished anything way beyond our abilities? Perhaps it's because we expect that accomplishment is always built on and surpassed. But just as a man 'peaks' and has his finest accomplishment, so do civilisations. Some humans write a book, paint a picture, climb a mountain or win a race, but can never go back and do it again. Through an amazing burst of excellence they 'push' something out, and then are content to recede and relinquish. So too with civilisations. No more pyramids for instance. The Polynesians had their finest hour of sea exploration, when for hundreds of years they honed skills that were later replaced by technology and western civilisation. Their scouts or navigators travelled across thousands of miles of ocean using a superior knowledge of the stars and ocean currents.[5] Their canoes were large enough to house the emigrants, their animals and enough food and water for weeks at sea.

It seems that civilisations from the North and South American continent were also travelling the Pacific Ocean. Proof of this lies with crops such as the sweet potato, which came from South America, but was dispersed all over Polynesia. According to Clive Ruggles, Emeritus Professor of Archaeoastronomy at the University of Leicester, the navigators were highly respected people who may have been chiefs or priests. They used stars at night, and kept a mental image of the rising and setting positions of key stars and star groups from any position in the sea. They would also take into account the Sun, winds, currents, swells and clouds. Seabirds would tell them of nearby land or they would follow their migratory paths.[6] Captain Cook himself used the service of one of these navigators. The final evidence came when modern adventurers made these journeys under the same conditions. In 1947 Thor Heyerdahl left the coast of South America in a copy of an ancient raft called the '*Kon Tiki*', arriving on a Polynesian island thousands of miles away, proving that early American civilisations could have had such a mastery of sailing. Then in 1975, a group called the Polynesian Voyaging Society also set out to prove what could be done and they launched a twin-hulled canoe in which they have sailed hundreds of thousands of miles throughout the Pacific Ocean using just sails and the stars. By 2007 this group had made many voyages, including a trip from Mangareva to Easter Island, a distance of some 1,450 miles, in only 19 days! The captain on that voyage said "We go to Rapa Nui in great humility and with respect for our ancestors, we go to rekindle the pride and dignity of our people and to reunite our ancient seafaring family."

After this historic journey one of the crew said "Surrounded by an immense sea and forced to turn inward, we had discovered a harmony within ourselves and with the natural world. For all of us, this voyage had been a rare gift of mana."[7]

Present day recognition of Makemake symbolises the revival of this deeply spiritual people and hopefully their reconnection to the souls of their ancestors, the sea, the stars and the birds.

In fairness to the scientific argument though, I need to point out that respected ecologists and scientists have sold many books on Easter Island to the public, declaring that "it is extremely improbable that the island could have been reached more than once before the arrival of the Europeans,"[8] and "The chances of two such voyages managing to reach the same isolated speck just by heading west beggars belief."[9]

I will leave the scientist's comments to the opinion of the reader.

There are hotly debated different theories as to which races colonised the island and when they did so. This type of disagreement and rivalry seems typical of the Polynesians and there are claims that around the 17th or 18th century the Islanders themselves had become quarrelsome.[10][11]

To give a short island history, accurate enough for our needs, I'll use that given by Thor Heyerdahl. It seems there were three epochs or periods. In the first, which lasted up to c.1200, explorers may have arrived from Chile or Peru bringing with them the skills to build massive platforms out of precisely cut huge stone blocks. American Indians were also colonising islands in the Pacific Ocean and could have reached Easter Island. There is evidence of Polynesian colonisation right at the beginning of the second period, circa 1200 to 1700.[12] One thing that is certain is that although the island was small, it was made up of several different cultures and tribes which remained separate. Most particularly, it seems as if there was a big east-west divide. During this second period the different tribes started to carve the giant stone statues out of a single quarry and erect them on the large stone platforms.

The third period between the 18th and 19th century saw a *very* sudden end to the statue carving. During this time the Europeans arrived bringing diseases, slavery and murder. The priests and island leaders were killed or abducted along with most of the population and the social structure and sacred spiritual beliefs were destroyed.

The island's timeline

First epoch 400 – 1200 AD Early explorers arrive at different times from places on the American continent. Perhaps early Peruvians, or American Indians and early Polynesian settlers. Huge stone platforms were built. A wave of Polynesian colonisers arrived around 1200.

Second epoch 1200 – 1700 Giant statues were carved. Rock carvings of Makemake made. Possibly some European landings in the 1600s, but no written records.

Third epoch 1722 – 1800s Dutch Admiral Roggeveen officially 'discovers' Easter Island and 12 Islanders are murdered, including their leader. Upright stone giants are seen. Population reported to be in the thousands. From then on, Americans and Europeans visit the island.

1570 – 1770 At some point there may have been tribal feuding.

1774 Captain Cook lands and calls it Easter Island. Evidence that some stone giants have fallen.

1840 – 1864 Last stone statue toppled?

1862 – 1863 A holocaust begins. Slave traders kidnap thousands.

1864 The first Christian missionary arrives. What's left of the population is dying from small pox, others were taken by missionaries to other islands.

1886 Official population count 157. William Thompson arrives on the 'Mohican' and stays for 12 days, writing the first reliable report.

1888 Chilean ownership.

1915 Official population count is 250.

Stories of the islands first Polynesian settlers

Island myths tell the story of how, in the first epoch, the first 300 or so Polynesian immigrants arrived on Easter Island. They were led over the sea by a king called Hotu Matu'a, who was escaping a bitter feud with a rival and had been advised by the great spirit Makemake that another island could be found.

Centuries passed and we entered the second epoch, at which point the island was divided between Hotu Matua's clans on the west side and another tribe known as the 'long ears' on the east side. (It was common for races in that area of the Pacific to make large holes in their earlobes by inserting increasingly larger items in them so that they eventually hung down to their shoulders.)

Towards the end of this epoch, there was tribal fighting between the clans and between east and west in particular. Legend has it that skirmishes, raids and assaults did occur between the clans, mainly over women, honour and territory. The issues over fidelity must have been of great importance because there are many stories involving women going off with other men and tribal war breaking out as a result, but it seems the Polynesian males regularly took part in war games and one-upmanship. William Thomson wrote of the Islanders in 1886 that:

> "Our guides were continually joking with each other, and we
> saw no quarreling or fighting. They are said to be brave and
> fearless of danger, but revengeful and savage when aroused."[13]

It is obvious that the earliest settlers were a resourceful, clever and courageous people, deeply respectful of Mother Earth, the spirits and their ancestral inheritance. Their way of life, competitive as it may have been, gave them something to be part of, they had a place, knew who they were and accepted both. Each clan had a class system of farmers, fishermen, priests, and royalty which supported their own statue carver's work. Early contact with the island found that it was well farmed with Islanders who were robust and good natured.

A record of the first contact, and the terrible outcome

The first recorded contact in 1722 describes how a single Islander in a canoe rowed out to a Dutch ship anchored three miles offshore. He was described as fit, strong and completely naked, except for a goatee beard, possibly a tribal leader. During his time on board he spoke at length to the heavens, (perhaps to the ancestors or Makemake?)

dancing and singing in gay merriment. When the Dutch landing party went ashore they were given a rapturous welcome, and the Islanders had gifts of roasted chicken and bananas ready for them. It is then reported that while the natives were exuding friendliness, (but also pilfering wood and cloth) trigger-happy sailors shot 12 of the Islanders, including the previously mentioned leader! The Islanders carried no weapons. Hours after the shootings, a chief dressed all in white quietly approached the Dutch offering homage and more bananas, sugar cane, young plants and chickens.[14] The Dutch left.

The next 140 years were no better

Can you imagine how people on planet Earth would be affected if aliens dropped from outer space and behaved in the same way that the Dutch did? This episode must have had a devastating effect on the Islanders. Subsequent explorers also put on big shows of firepower and gun salutes, which the Islanders were terrified of. Such was the impact that centuries later, with no written history to refer to, the island's verbal legends still faithfully described all of these early encounters with outsiders. One contemporary author reports that:

> "from 1722 to 1863 more than 1,000 Islanders were gunned down or transported to their death by Europeans, North Americans and South Americans."[15]

It must have been at this point that the Islanders took to living in underground caves to hide from these raids. Thor Heyerdahl found evidence of this in the 1950s.

The sexual freedom of the Islanders

The women of Easter Island were famous for their beauty and grace. They wore no clothes and enjoyed their seductive prowess and eroticism. Their attitude to sexuality was very different to ours. It was not taboo and they understood it to be a truly creative act that celebrated fecundity and the abundance of life. This went down well with the European and American sailors who sailed the Pacific at that time and the Islanders mostly gave them a hearty welcome. From 1820 to 1860 hundreds of whaling ships called at Easter Island, mainly for the huge pleasure the women could give the men. Crews found the Islanders to be docile and the females sexually inviting. (According to island practice, women could be leased out to other men. It had probably become necessary when there were fewer women than men in the early days. There would be trouble though, if the lady in question chose to look even further afield!)

Visiting sailors would have left behind diseases, Christian doctrine, pregnancies and maybe even the odd crew member, since the women were so keen to engage with these status-enhancing males. It is worth noting that throughout all the sailors' reports the worst atrocity any Islander committed against the explorers was to throw stones and steal. A report in *New Scientist* in 2006 said that artifacts previously identified as spearheads were actually agricultural implements and only a third of these had sharp edges.[16] This article also quotes an extract written in a French journal in 1786, "a considerable population, with more beauty and grace than I afterwards met with on any other island;" So it was disturbing to read a report about an American whaling ship called the Pindos in 1822. Island girls were taken on board for an all night orgy, but the next morning they were thrown into the sea. The crowd that then gathered on the beach were shot at.

White skin was revered and apparently quite prevalent among the Islanders. This was often commented on by the early explorers who were mystified by it.

Polynesian men had an exploring, fighting, macho image, and respected strong leadership. If their leaders were perceived as weak compared with the destructive might of the white aliens, then that leadership could be challenged. This might have brought about inter-island rivalry. When the island women gave birth to white skinned

10 *This is a copy of a drawing done by a member of Captain Cook's party in 1774. Note the European type features and the elongated ear lobes*

males, courtesy of the Europeans or Americans, they were naturally challenging to the island's royalty. Their shamans, chiefs and ancestral spirits had had undisputed authority, but that old system was crumbling, since the higher authority now was the white man with his guns, cloth and wood. Makemake was losing his ground.

The power and authority of their own leaders would have been brought into question when compared to the brutal 'magic' of these new white warriors and this would have caused a crisis of faith and leadership, so it is no surprise that some books suggest that tribal fighting broke out again around this time.

Another factor that may have changed the Islanders way of life after first contact was their mimicry. They saw the way the foreigners behaved and copied it. Commentators throughout the years have commented on the islander's amenability and eagerness to please.

Thieving came naturally to the Islanders and they frequently stole from each other. It was a way of life, and no shame in it and they even had a god to oversee it. They stole hats from the sailors and these were important to the Islanders, since headdress denoted authority. (The chiefs and kings wore impressive head-dresses made from bird's feathers.) The Islanders had secret family caves where things could be kept safe from thieves. The caves were protected by very elaborate rituals. Signs of cannibalism were found in them in 1955.

The holocaust that decimated the population

The holocaust happened between 1862 and 1886, and it reduced the island's population from thousands to 155. In one recorded incident alone, Peruvians took up to 1,500 Islanders as labourers, one of them being the king. Most quickly succumbed to homesickness and diseases that their immune system could not cope with.[17] It has recently been discovered that the soil of the island contains a special life-enhancing substance called Rapamycin and perhaps they couldn't live without it. Anyway, after international condemnation, it was decided to return the survivors to the island. Only a handful survived the journey and the smallpox disease they carried with them started an epidemic that nearly wiped out the remaining Islanders. (If you're not crying yet, you must be a Scorpio!)

Two French Catholic missionaries were sent to the island in 1866, one of whom frowned on Makemake and the yearly 'birdman' competition in his honour. Sexual practices, idols and ritual performances were all forbidden.[18] The word for penis was replaced by the word for wickedness and all singing and dancing was stopped. In an attempt to rid the island of its spiritual heritage they ordered the burning of all the tablets carved with ancient island hieroglyphs, and the destruction of all pagan idols. European entrepreneurs then took over the stricken island, wrote themselves contracts of ownership, fought bitterly with each other and finally turned the island into a sheep ranch. A different and more sympathetic missionary left for another island, taking many of the inhabitants with him. A census in 1886 reported 157 people living on the island, with the even lower figure of 111 in 1872.[19] I guess I don't need to say any more than that!

What was left of old Easter Island and Makemake

The Islanders had suffered a reduction of their numbers through slave raids and imported diseases. Their king had been captured and the heart and soul had been taken out of their culture. Thomson wrote:

> "Maurata, the last of a long line of kings, together with all
> of the principal chiefs of the islands was kidnapped by the
> Peruvians and died in slavery. Since that time there has been
> no recognised authority among the natives; every man is his
> own master, and looks out for his own interests."[20]

So the few remaining Islanders became directionless and vulnerable, as if the soul and spirit of the people had died along with their leaders and belief system. The final 'death' of Makemake came when the first missionaries announced sexuality and pagan gods to be evil.

William Thomson remarked that "The amusements of the people were reduced to a minimum when the customs of their heathen forefathers were abandoned."[21]

William Thomson's report for the National Museum 1891

The report was written by a seemingly observant, thorough and humorous chap. In 1886 he was a paymaster of the US Navy and spent 12 days over Christmas on Easter Island writing a long and detailed report for the United States National Museum, and it is the earliest and most reliable account we have. He arrived about 20 years after the holocaust and spoke to important survivors of it. Other scholars arrived later, but by then all the survivors had died and there was no written record. Thomson has been accused of ransacking ancient, archeologically interesting ruins, but he comes over as a precise and gentle man who wrote a very detailed document that gives us tremendous insight into the people, their culture and their history. He suffered considerable discomfort at times, but throughout this meticulous and studious report a wickedly dry sense of humour is evident. This description of his encounters with the insects demonstrates this humour:

> "From the earliest dawn of day to the close of the short twilight… swarms of flies met us, prepared to dispute every foot of the ground. Whatever may have been the parent stock of the Polynesians, we came to the unanimous conclusion that we had discovered here the lineal descendants of the flies that composed the Egyptian plague, and can testify that they have not degenerated in the lapse of time. Fleas occasioned us more annoyance than the flies, because this industrious little insect was untiring in its attentions by day and night. They were found in numbers in all the camping places, and we seemed to get a fresh supply every time a halt was called."[22]

He was the only one who gave the island its real name and said that no one else had thought to ask the natives what they called their home.

At the end of this chapter I have included a quote from William Thomson because I think it gives an insight into the soul of the man who wrote so carefully and thoughtfully of Easter Island.

Taboo and mana

The spiritual system of Polynesia rests on these two principles and most especially so on Easter Island. Mana is a supernatural power that can be wielded only by certain people, or can be won by those who go about things in the right way. These days we use the term 'good karma', which is not unlike a watered down mana. On Easter Island, the priests were the custodians of mana, but it could be found wherever things were going well; it meant they had been imbued with mana or good magic. Mana could also reside in a simple or sacred object.

Taboo refers to something that is not allowed. Taboo can be placed in objects that are left to warn people off, or it can be passed on by a verbal warning. The Islanders lived their lives wholly and completely according to taboo and mana and it would rule such things as crop protection and bans on fishing to protect spawning fish.

The Islander's spiritual beliefs

The Islanders believed that a person's soul went to a spirit land that contained neither reward nor retribution; it just existed. Holes were built into burial places to let the soul out. Good and bad spirits also existed, they wandered the Earth and had influence over human lives, and could also communicate through dreams and visions. Some spirits became personal guardians to be called upon for guidance. Stone carvings in a variety of images represented a different genre of spirits or household gods and these could be consulted, but they weren't worshipped. They were simply an access portal to the other dimension of spirits. William Thomson found recesses for the statues of these household gods built into the construction of the earliest houses. He wrote down translations of Island hieroglyphs that give everything in existence an associated spirit or deity, from rocks to yams, grass, pain, bad smells, sea gulls, stars, luck and life! All things were imbued with a spiritual force, and a dialogue could go between humans and this energy.

The Islanders were controlled by superstitions and fear of the spirit world and its supernatural power. To this end, they worked ceaselessly to appease the invisible forces, always trying to work in harmony with them. Fishhooks were made from the bones of dead fishermen in an effort to invoke their spiritual support and skill. Carved stones were buried under the threshold of dwellings to ward off evil spirits, and their priests, before the arrival of Christianity, would have been skilled in communicating with the spirit world, invoking magic, power and healing from it. The harmful spirits could invoke such paralysing fear that no one ever crossed them.

Makemake was in a class of his own. He was the Great Spirit, and when Islanders understood that Europeans were praying, they joined in with cries to "Meke-meke".[23] Here in the western world, some of us are comforted by the belief that the spirit or soul of a loved one lives on in the 'other side' or 'in spirit' and it comforts us to think we can still talk to them. The Easter Islanders whole-heartedly embraced this belief and took it to a much higher level. The ancestral spirits were protectors, guardians, masters, guides and constant companions to be consulted with in everything. We have translations of prayers that were offered to them to encourage abundance in health, food production and pregnancy, amongst other things.[24] The prayers mention the giant platforms, which were built before the statues and positioned around the coast. They look like giant outdoor stages but were actually catacombs that held the bones of the ancestors. The statues were carved as a reminder and in honour of these ancestors, perpetuating their memory and keeping their protection fresh and strong. The prayers said the spirits of the ancestors were "in the Sun", but they were also accessible to the living as protectors and benefactors. This reference to the Sun does not have to mean Sun worship. The element of fire is a metaphor for the invisible realm of spirit, the life force of another dimension that underpins ours. In astrology the physical Sun is one of the things that represents spirit.

Ancient spiritual hieroglyphs called Rongorongo

In 1864 the first Christian missionary arrived and saw that surviving Islanders had stone or wooden tablets written in an ancient script called Rongorongo, which they kept in their houses and clearly treasured. The missionary, however, decided to rid the small remaining population of its pagan beliefs, resulting in the destruction of nearly all the Rongorongo texts. Only 20 pieces or so have survived.

The hieroglyphs of the script feature figures, animals and objects, with a significant number of fish and miniature so-called 'birdmen' figures, often the same shape as the larger ones carved on the rocks.

11 *Copy of the Easter Island hieroglyphs called Rongorongo script*

The figures aren't the same as the Egyptian ones, but it is a similar concept and birds appear in both.

The Polynesians never developed a writing system, so unless we consider ancient myths of sunken islands and lost civilisations we are left with the mystery of where it came from. In 1939 a learned scholar claimed the hieroglyphs had similarities with some found in India, but this was scoffed at. Island myth states that tablets of the script were carried over the sea by the original pioneers. Thomson found a very old specimen of it in an ancient tomb[25] so it is not a recent thing. But if *where* this writing came from is a mystery, then *what it means* is an even bigger one!

The script is carved in relief and when you reach the end of a line you have to turn the tablet as the next line is upside down to the first. This puzzles the experts but it seems to me that it would make it easier to read in the dark. If you are feeling it then you can't loose your place and skip a line if alternate lines are upside down. This would have come in handy for reading it in the caves at night or on a long sea voyage.

Information gleaned by Thomson suggests that the text contains original myths and hymns that would have been important to their rituals and spiritual well-being. There are lists of gods and goddesses together with their parentage and earthly associations, for instance. Recent scholars believe they have the key to reading this text, but since all such knowledge died along with the royal families and priests, no one will ever be able to confirm this. The writer Steven Fischer thinks that one of the texts is solely about procreation, noting who copulated with who to produce what. There may be an emphasis on the male phallus and sex. According to Sergei Rjabchikov,[26] head of the Research Centre for Studies of Ancient Civilisations and Cultures, another text refers to water, darkness, burning, raining and different phases of the Moon. There are references to Makemake as a Sun god, along with the rising, setting and eclipses of the Sun. He believes there is information on Hailey's comet and a solar eclipse in 1531.

There is much discussion and evidence regarding this on many of the Rongorongo websites for those who would like further information.

Longevity, herbs and the mysterious 'Lomilomi' healing method

Apparently one male Islander who reached the age of 125, had milk white hair, could scarcely walk and had 23 children[27], although not necessarily in that order! Thor Heyerdahl spoke of one who was 108 years old and William Thomson also comments on the longevity of the Islanders; two of those known to him being in their nineties When they weren't being murdered or kidnapped, the Islanders lived a long time!

Thomson observed that the 155 remaining Islanders were in good health, apart from the occasional cold and cracked feet from walking on rocks. He suggested that physical regeneration came about through a healing therapy called Lomi-lomi. He wrote:

"I may testify to the physical regeneration of this (pleasurable) manipulation. On more than one occasion I have thrown myself upon the ground, completely exhausted by over-exertion, and yielded to the dextrous kneadings and frictions and palmings and pinchings of those skilled in the treatment. The hard fisted native is by no means gentle in the operation, but with palms and knuckles vigorously tests every muscle and tendon, as well as every joint of the vertebrae until the exhausted patient sinks into oblivious somnolence."[28]

The practitioner claimed that this in itself wasn't enough, he was also applying "occult knowledge and supernatural power". This must be similar to reiki, which has its origins in Polynesia. The Lomi-lomi by itself did not cause the longevity, but the free and copious use of it plus a healthy seafood diet must have contributed to a long life.

However, scientists also discovered a chemical called Rapamycin, in the soil and rock, which has incredible life enhancing properties. There is now a race to prepare it for testing with the hope that it will cure many degenerative diseases.

There is an island story that demonstrates just how resilient and strong the men were. During the raiding and kidnapping of 1805 an American vessel kidnapped groups of Islanders after a ruthless and bloody encounter.[29] After three days of sailing they allowed the victims on deck and immediately the men sprang overboard. It was assumed they all drowned and the incident was simply written into the ship's log. But island legends gathered by missionary Sebastian Englert in the 20th century reported this story. How could the Islanders know this? Certainly the ship did not return to report it. The legend came from one of the survivors who swam back to the island! He had survived the raid, three days in the hold of a ship and then a long swim home. Upon his return, his amazing story had become one of the island's legends.

The "festival of the seabirds eggs"

The early Europeans arrived to find an annual competition that tested the strength, courage and stamina of the Island men. Thomson called it the "festival of the seabirds eggs" while contemporary writers call it the 'birdman' competition. It centred on a steep cliff between the sea and a volcanic crater in a corner of the island called Orongo. On the day of the winter solstice, which is June 21st in the southern hemisphere, the rising Sun just happens to line up exactly with Orongo and the volcano at the other end of the Island.[30] The winter solstice has always been a very important spiritual occasion for pagans the world over. It marks the shortest day in the winter and the beginning of the Sun's return to power. From this point on the Sun gains in strength and nature begins the march towards spring and summer, symbolising re-birth and regeneration.[31]

On Easter Island the winter solstice also marked the beginning of the season in which the treasured sooty tern returned. Islanders would go to Orongo and wait for the arrival of the birds who came to lay their eggs on an offshore islet. The men would then climb down the cliff, navigate the dangerous stretch of water on a small raft made of reeds, climb up onto the rocky islet, collect an egg, and finally carry it back unbroken. Thomson wrote:

> "According to the ancient custom, the fortunate individual who obtained possession of the first egg and returned with it unbroken to the expectant crowd, became entitled to certain privileges and rights during the following year. No especial authority was vested in him, but it was supposed that he had won the approval of the great spirit Makemake and was entitled to receive contributions of food and other considerations from his fellows."

According to Thomson anyone could enter, and factional fighting was common. Many writers since Thomson have written different versions of this, but as I said before, he took his notes from the surviving 157 Islanders and it is the most accurate record. Subsequent accounts may have been embellished, since the Islanders loved giving the person in front of them a good story!

Associated with this competition is a symbol called a 'birdman', which has different forms and is carved on many of the rocks at Orongo.

These have earlier and later forms and many carvings are imposed

*12 and 13 Rock carvings and paintings of the birdman symbol.
If you see the beaks as ears, they look more like rabbits to me!*

over previous ones (see above). Alongside the birdman images is that of a mask, supposedly depicting Makemake (see page 119). Thomson sees this Great Spirit as the patron saint of the competition.

While the island's rock art is extremely prevalent around Orongo, it also exists in abundance elsewhere. Often the images carved are the same as those in the Rongorongo script but which came first is unknown.

The images sometimes bear resemblance to sea creatures and sometimes to constellations and stars, since without light pollution and high buildings the night sky would have been the most dominant feature of the Islanders lives. The position of certain stars at different times of the year gave them information about weather and planting that was vital to food production.

A large boulder, found in a volcano crater, was carved with strange, spiritually imbued sea creatures, one of which had a human-like head. Possibly one of Makemake's earliest images, showing his origins as the Great Sea Spirit.

Tricksters and thieves

The island rock art has an extremely strange quality. It can change into a different image when you look at it a different way. The mask of Makemake shown on page 119 is actually a man's genital region when viewed upside down. The birdman images can look like rabbits if you see the stylised beak as ears. The giant statues are just that until you notice how they are carved in the shape of the male phallus. This is more symbolism to add to the changing nature of this culture. The Islanders obviously adored trickery and it must have been a good defence system for them. They had extremely impressionable natures, so their competitive rivalry was played out in subtle ways. They were extremely adept at picking pockets, but they weren't aggressive enough to steal guns, so they stole items such as hats and handkerchiefs. When they traded with the Europeans, the sailors would find that a basket of sweet potatoes was actually a bag of stones with a few potatoes on top.

They had a god to assist them in thieving whose name was Hiro and he was also the god of rain in Polynesia. Complex rules governed what was allowed and what wasn't, but if someone transgressed then they had to submit to physical abuse from the victim without retaliating. Submission and acceptance were features of the Islanders mentality. Once this punishment was over, the matter was forgotten.

Interestingly the planet Makemake was going to be called Manabozho at one point, and he was a rabbit trickster god.

The Stone Giants

Most people are aware of the giant stone statues of Easter Island. These are huge monoliths, carved out of one piece of volcanic rock and transported to the island's three coasts to be placed on pre-existing large platforms, which were catacombs for the bones of the ancestors. On average they are 13 feet high, weigh 14 tons and most face inwards, with their backs to the sea. On the south coast alone there are 17 platforms in just two miles. A lot of the statues also had different hats carved out of red volcanic rock from a separate part of the island. Although these weigh many tons, the Islanders placed them on top of the statues.

14 *Mo'ai or stone statues of Easter Island. They were intended to stand on giant platforms as shown. They were on the coast but looked inward, towards the islanders*

There are roughly 800 statues altogether with about half still in the production centre or quarry in one of the volcanoes. Some 300 had actually been transported to their coastal destinations, but about 50 were waiting to begin their journey and 50 were en route.[32]

In his book *Aku-Aku*, Thor Heyerdahl wrote of how he wandered about in the production centre in the side of the volcano, with 400 unfinished giants silently watching him. Most puzzling was the abandoned stone picks that the workers had used to painstakingly chip away at the volcanic rock. They had thrown their tools down one day and never gone back. Thomson said:

"The images in all stages of incompletion in the workshops, and abandoned en route to the coast in various directions, indicate, that the work was suddenly arrested, and not gradually brought to an end."[33]

One theory suggests that the carving stopped upon the arrival of the Europeans. Perhaps their murderous behaviour implied that the protective power of the ancestors associated with the giants was not working, so producing more became futile? Or did the arrival of the Europeans spark off island feuding and tribal leadership issues, which took the work force away from the quarry? Was the statue factory manager one of the Islanders who was shot in the first contact? Or was it a combination of things?

One report states that each tribe had its own road to where it lived on the island, and there were seven different roads. In terms of the man power available, and the massive amount of construction that took place, the Islanders invested more time and energy per person than any other culture in the ancient world involved in the production of giant megalithic structures.[34] It is estimated that it took about 500 years to do this amount of work and they could have been constructing them up to the 1700s. However, another commentator, Fischer, thought they may have been in production from 1250 to 1500. One thing is clear and that is they were getting bigger. The most recent was up to 28 feet tall, weighing perhaps 75 tons. The increase in size may have been one-upmanship. "My statue's bigger than your statue!"

Although the Islanders had an intensely competitive instinct and strongly individual tribal identity, they must have co-operated in the carving of these giants. Apparently a great deal of tribal pride and dignity was invested. The statues were built to impress and protect.

Certainly the statues represented and honoured the spirits of the ancestors in a yang or masculine image, although there were a handful of female forms. Although they all looked roughly the same, there were some differences brought about by the carvers and clans involved. Thomson reported that surviving Islanders knew the names of each statue, and he tested them individually to be sure. He said they were "effigies of distinguished persons and intended as monuments to perpetuate memory."[35] He points out that they were not idols and were not worshipped. The Islanders did not confuse them with actual gods. Importantly, although they carved many different wooden and stone images, there didn't seem to be any mini mo'ai statues and they never carved mo'ai faces on the rocks. A translator of Rongorongo said the text consisted of prayers to the good guardian spirits of the ancestors who were powerful protectors and represented by the "sacred stone pillars" or stone giants.[36]

When reading island mythology it is obvious that the similarity to the shape of the male phallus is intentional. The people's love of the male erection and the prowess and dominance associated with it was built into all their cultural expressions. Carved lines representing the hands and fingers of the statues emphasised and cradled its male genitals.

Scholars like to guess at how these sacred stone pillars were moved miles from the quarry across the island and on this the island myths were emphatic. They 'walked'. The Islanders solemnly reported to Thomson that the statues walked about in the dark, assisted their clans in competition and could prophesise.

We do not know why they were positioned on the coasts facing inwards. They obviously weren't erected to frighten off those approaching the island. They were enclosing the island, forming a protective circle around it. They looked out over the people and the people could look up and see the representatives of their ancestors looking back. As suggested by the name of the island, ('navel at the centre of the world' or 'navel of the deep') the statues were contemplating the island's own navel.

Why then, were they knocked down in later years? The main theory is that the Islanders pushed each other's statues over to nullify the ancestral power or upset their neighbours during tribal skirmishes. Theory number two involves a legend called 'The Fall of The Stone Statues'. In it, we are told, "The statues fell to the ground. The wind blew, there was lightning, thunder rumbled in the night. The next day the statues had fallen."[37] Interesting that there should be a story about them being brought down by a storm, when surely the more exciting story would have been about warrior wars and heroes. It just so happens that in 1746 the most deadly earthquake and tsunami for 200 years destroyed the entire port of Callao and city of Lima on the coast of Peru, which is the land closest to Easter Island.[38] While looking at one particular platform, William Thomson noted that:

> "The ruined condition of these solid specimens of architecture, with the overthrown images and immense deposit of loose boulders on the surface of the ground, are strongly suggestive of earthquakes and volcanic eruption."[39]

Such an earthquake happened again in 1960, and the resulting 26 feet high tsunami carried 15 statues, weighing approx. 30 tons each, for 500 feet inland,[40] so it obviously happens. (There is a question mark over the deity responsible for the tsunami of 2004 and at this point the jury is still out as to whether Makemake or Sedna have patronage.)

Perhaps the two theories can be combined and tribal leadership upheavals happened as an earthquake felled some of the statues and this started a spate of retaliatory statue felling. We are never going to know for sure. The silent statues will keep their secrets for eternity.

Where does the god Makemake come from and what does he represent?

The word Makemake contains a duplication of one word and this is apparently an emphasis, a superlative implying a higher degree of quality. Thomson was told Meke-meke was 'the Great Spirit of the Sea' and certainly the earliest images of him implied he swam in the sea or moved in the ether.

Makemake's prominence as creator god of fertility belongs to Easter Island only. Just 64 square miles of planet Earth. The usual chief Polynesian gods weren't especially acknowledged. According to legend, one of them called Hiro, god of rain and thieves was accepted. Another of them, Tangara, arrived but was murdered on the beach. It was thought that two others may have been merged into Makemake. But in truth, it is a mystery! How and why did the Islanders have a god that didn't appear anywhere else?

Sometimes the need for a certain god or goddess is driven by a surplus or lack of something in that culture. The sensitivity of a population anywhere to the lack of water for instance, or the abundance of seafood, will guide them to identify deities that can represent these matters. Another thing that influences the relevance of local gods and goddesses is the sky above. Ancient civilisations the world over used the moving canopy of the night sky and planets as their television, newspaper and Internet. And just as these things influence our lives now, so the busy and vibrant stars influenced the ancients. The gods and goddesses were and are represented by stars and planets which look as if they are moving around and stories were concocted to explain the effect this would have on people's lives. Now take a look again at the map of Polynesia at the front of this chapter. The distance from Hawaii to Easter Island is 4,600 miles, which is more than the distance from England to Alaska, but more importantly the sky that can be seen on a regular yearly basis in the northern hemisphere (Hawaii) is *different* to the view from the southern hemisphere (Easter Island). Different stars were rising and falling just before the all-important sunrise. Stars that rose ahead of the Sun were *most* important to *all* the ancient civilisations. Now put all that together and it is easy to see why different Polynesian islands (Hawaii and Easter Island) had some differing deities. The needs, outlook and culture of the people were different.

Because Easter Island sits between Tahiti (Polynesia) and Chile (South America), it was and is a fusion of east and west. Largely because of the sea travel undertaken by the early Americans and Polynesians in the first millennium, some things such as the habit of lengthening earlobes, plants such as the sweet potato and bottle gourd, and megalithic stone work was prevalent throughout this area. Important early cities, found in both South America and on Easter Island had names that roughly meant the "Navel of the Earth". DNA from chicken bones found in Chile and dated to 1400 had the same DNA as those found on two South Pacific islands even further away than Easter Island.[41]

Easter Island was where the influence of Polynesia and the Americas fused. The Polynesian influence was stronger, but the South American influence was just enough to make some things unique to Easter Island only. So enter Makemake, unheard of in South America or Polynesia. An ingenious and mysterious Easter Island solution to the presence of two great spiritual dynasties and local needs. There were some similarities between the spiritual beliefs of the Peruvians and the Polynesians. The ancient Peruvians also deeply revered their ancestors and as the number of ancestors increased, so did the ritual demands. Both races recognised the importance of a cluster of stars called the Pleiades, which used to rise before the Sun in the morning.[42]

To understand this, you have to imagine what it was like to be entirely dependent on the success of your own crops. There was no going to the local supermarket if your potatoes failed to grow. You lived or died according to the success of the crops you were planting. Because the ancients had no weather forecasts they used a more reliable method. They watched the stars! The island's priesthood knew that if the Pleiades looked dim around the winter solstice they needed to plant at a different time to adjust for the coming season of reduced rainfall. Scientific research carried out in 1999 proved this to be true. The poor visibility is caused by a different pattern in very high clouds, which changes the weather pattern for the growing season seven months hence.[43]

Easter Island had no source of fresh water, and rainfall quickly drained away through the volcanic rock and myriad caves. So their all-important potato crops depended on a planting strategy that made best use of the coming rain. Their neighbours in South America had this forecasting system and it would have been passed on to the island's

priests and elders by explorers going back and forth. The brightness
of the Pleiades on the date of the winter solstice would have told them
when to plant to take best advantage of next season's rainfall.

Easter Island has a natural cliff top feature which would tell the
Islanders when the exact day of the winter solstice was, and the
priesthood couldn't have failed to notice that the season of the return
of the seabirds to lay eggs was also heralded by this day. Makemake's
image was carved all over this feature, and the 'Festival of the Seabirds
Eggs' was arranged around it. This date must have also influenced
the seasonal ban on fishing imposed by the priests to allow stocks to
breed. Turtles were regarded as sacred, as many rock carvings testify,
and they also have ancient symbolism with the Pleiades. They, like
seabirds, crossed thousands of miles to lay eggs on Easter Island and
they were protected by the taboo of the priesthood, which meant the
number killed was strictly controlled. Turtles bridged the two worlds
of deep sea and land and as such could be messengers of the Great
Sea Spirit, one of Makemake's titles. They could also assist souls to
the next dimension. Their egg laying cycle depended on new and full
Moons, which the priests could predict.[44]

A clue to Makemake's origins comes from Polynesian mythology
containing a lesser-known deity called Makalii or Makarika. The
Pleiades (along with another group of stars called Hyades) were known
as Makalii or Makalii's nets. (There is a myth that a Polynesian rat
gnawed through these nets, but she wasn't in trouble because she was
Makalii's sister.)[45]

It is easy to see how Makarika became Makemake and usurped the
usual Polynesian creator god who may not have been practical enough
for Easter Island needs. They needed a creator god of abundance and
fertility to join Hiro, god of rainfall, who was also connected with the
star cluster of Pleiades. It is also easy to see how this happened when
we understand that this all-important information about the weather
could mean the difference between a bumper crop and a failed one.

It would mean life and death on an island with no fresh water and a sexually indulgent population who enjoyed procreating.

But although the Pleiades and the winter solstice were of crucial importance for timing purposes, the real spiritual support and power for growth and re-generation came from Makemake. Perhaps he was actually Rapamycin, the chemical or elixir of life found recently in the soil. If the Islanders knew that this substance gave them life-enhancing qualities, then they would have thought that gift to be deity.

What did Makemake look like?

William Thomson gave us the most important Makemake image, but I seem to be the only one who thinks so! This may be because his report did not become a book and was not readily available to the public. Since then, scholars have concerned themselves with other issues such as statue erection and ecology, and knowledge of Makemake has been consigned to one or two brief mentions in Easter Island books in which they use one of the many birdman carvings to represent him.

However, William Thomson says "According to the natives, this symbol was intended to represent the god 'Meke Meke', the great spirit of the sea." He then refers to his own drawing:

15 A copy of an illustration drawn by William Thomson in 1886. This image was carved on a rock

118

"The general outline of this figure, rudely carved upon the rocks, bore a striking resemblance to the decoration on a piece of pottery which I once dug up in Peru, while making excavations among the graves of the Incas. The form is almost identical, but except for this instance, no similarity was discovered between the relics of Easter Island and the coast of South America."

I then spent a very long night trying to find similar images on the Internet. I eventually found two, but that hardly constitutes prevalence, so I decided that I'm going to go to the South Pacific to carve something silly on a rock for someone to find in 2,000 years. It'll drive them mad!

The Islanders didn't make pottery, so none could have been taken to Peru. The explanation has to be that one or two items with this image on made their way *from* Peru. William Thomson sketched his Makemake image over 120 years ago and it may have eroded since then, because it is not used in the recent Easter Island books. However this face is very similar to that of an early epoch statue unearthed by Thor Heyerdahl in the 1950s. Thomson's ghostly image is so ethereal and ambiguous, it suggests many different possibilities and perhaps that is the point. It is all things; neither a land animal, nor a sea creature or a spirit from another realm. Makemake is everything. At some point the face of this image was reduced to a mask, and masks of one form or another are common in Polynesia.

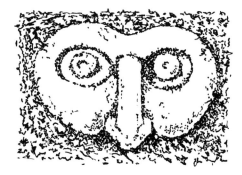

16 This 'mask' rock carving of Makemake is the more recent and most prevalent image of him

However, nowadays Makemake is associated with the more modern of the birdman images (see page 109) which are superimposed over the earlier, more spirit-like and ethereal images. The silhouette of the birdman has similarities with those on other Polynesian islands.

So there it is, the very earliest image of Makemake, with evidence that seems to point to a Peruvian connection as well as a Polynesian pedigree.

The meaning of Makemake to the Islanders

Makemake the Great Sea Spirit

These days, it is said that Makemake was the creator of humanity, the god of fertility and the chief god of the birdman ritual. Thomson said the survivors called him the Great Sea Spirit, and implied he had a close connection with the ocean. This is only natural since the island was surrounded by sea. It seems that this ocean was more abundant than we previously realised and the Islanders had a lot to thank Makemake for. In 2008 it was reported in *New Scientist* that the area north of Easter Island had been found to be one of the best places on Earth for large ocean predatory fish such as marlin, tuna and shark.[46] This has surprised the scientists who put it down to a perfect sea temperature.

Another remarkable report came out in 2009, when scientists found that storms or changes to the usual annual weather events of the eastern Pacific had a dramatic impact on the quantity of important fish *years* after the event. This is due to the nutrients that get brought up from deep water, boosting stocks and breeding potential. It says "The effect of El Nino on fish has probably been observed for millennia" and:

> "After discovering these relationships between decades long fluctuations in fish and climate all over the world, scientists are now probing back in time to see if similar relationships exist on the order of centuries and millennia."[47]

So storms and tsunamis look likely to improve the amount of available seafood over the following years. It is possible that the Islanders attributed these extreme weather events to Makemake, since he was the Great Sea Spirit and capable of creating them.

Another of his great gifts to the Islanders was 'The Festival of the Seabirds' which revolved around the winter solstice and was used to judge the brightness of the star cluster called the Pleiades. As I said earlier, this would describe the strength and timing of the El Nino rainfall and winds the following year, and tell them the best time to plant. They were guided by the priests, who understood nature's way and how to work with sea conditions and projected breeding patterns and who then used taboo to control planting and fishing. The Islanders were able to enjoy Makemake's abundance while living with nature. If they observed the festivals, traditions and social restrictions, the Islanders would have good crops, birds eggs and prolific seafood. Perhaps the recently discovered Rapamycin chemical also boosted the virility, stamina and profusion of everything on the island. The problems came with the breakdown of the social order and loss of spiritual connection that taboo, mana and the priesthood had kept in good working order. The murder, slavery and island holocaust replaced the priests who could 'read' the brightness of Pleiades and enforce the ritual taboo that protected the people. Makemake's importance was *really* lost when the island population was reduced to 111 survivors, none of whom were priests or elders themselves.

Makemake as a sexually bawdy deity

Father Sebastian, a later island missionary and a deeply spiritual man, explained how Makemake began as one thing and changed into another and I think there is no doubt that whatever Makemake was in the first millennium, in the 19th century he was a sexually bawdy and competitive deity. This had much to do the properties of

Rapamycin, although it was also completely in keeping with the competitive macho image that was prevalent at the time.

World myths often tell us of how new ways open up when things are looking bad. Populations somehow find the will to go on because of the arrival of a bawdy joker who brings humour, mirth or at the very least distraction, just when the lowest ebb is reached.[48] Sexual innuendo or lascivious comments are common and Makemake fits right into this role. Such a story can be found on the Marquesas Islands, which are Polynesian islands close to Easter Island. It can also be found in the mythology of Greece, Japan and Egypt, which shows how myths seem to be hard-wired into our DNA and emerge when triggered by a certain event.[49] When the Islanders had all but been wiped out of existence, Makemake became a rich source of bawdy sexual innuendo, which was useful both as a reminder to procreate and replace the lost population, but also to provide something to snigger about. Makemake was naturally equipped to provide the sexually suggestive innuendo because he had serious connections to sex in the first place. Maybe his energy *is* the Rapamycin. William Thomson points out that the Rongorongo script contains much reference to Makemake and the female vulva, which represents the birth of a person.

The Rongorongo script seemingly contains lots of reference to deity and the creation, and since the small figures are similar to the rock art that Islanders identify as Makemake, some assume the god of the hieroglyphs is Makemake. The following was written by a scholar in an article printed in the Journal of the Polynesian Society in 1939.

"It was perhaps the emphasis on sexuality in these tablets that made the basis of the Easter Island belief in their virtue as aids to conception. There are other religious cues of the characters; the great god Makemake is very often repeated; it is made of bird, mammal, sometime human and fish; it takes varieties of forms. He is the representative of power; he is seated on his throne, with symbols of royal authority in his hands; his head touches the heavens and he wields the lightning and thunder".[50] "Makemake's energy supported numerous different forms of emotions connected with procreation and fecundity. He was a stimulation to fertility, impregnated with the passion of procreation and the idea of reproduction, which was never out of the minds of the people."[51]

A more recent theory suggests that in old Rapanui language Makemake means "tumescent (of the phallus)", meaning swollen or becoming swollen.[52]

To get a better impression of the prowess and abundance that Makemake can endow we need to take into account the easily expressed feelings of Mike Brown, the planet's discoverer. His wife was pregnant at the time and his male pride was apparent for all to see when he talked of his wife's pregnancy and the birth of his daughter.

Physical prowess and competition

According to Thomson, Makemake was celebrated at the important island festivals through sporting competition. Events such as stone, javelin, and net throwing or the annual race and swim to collect the birds eggs were common and the Islanders loved them. The celebrations would revolve around such events as changes in the seasons or the anniversary of the arrival of the mythical first king. Losers easily resigned themselves to their fate and whatever loss they had to bear. It is a remarkable that the nature of the Islanders and their spiritual beliefs meant that they happily surrendered to that which prevailed.

Birds as sacred beings and messengers of the divine

Headdresses made of feathers denoted rank or statesmanship as it did in many cultures in that part of the world. Birds had supreme importance in all the major spiritual dynasties. A glance through Egyptian, North

American Indian and Eskimo mythology will testify to this, to mention just a few. Birds held a special place because they could communicate with the sky gods and goddesses and the people on Earth, and they could carry the soul into the other realms. They would disappear for months and then reappear to nest and lay eggs, so it was no wonder that the Islanders associated them with travel to other realms and the return to Earth to begin a new cycle. The Easter Islanders venerated them and used them to navigate thousands of miles across the ocean.

The magic of shells and feathers

Shells and feathers were given the highest reverence as ornamentation, with only island kings and priests wearing certain types, with others being reserved for special events. The spirit of the sea creature or bird remained in its bones or shell or feathers, so giving the means to be closely identified with these sacred and spiritual representatives. As feathers and shells protect their occupants, so they might confer the power of protection to their new wearer. Such was their belief that the power of the spirit remained in the bone, they would make fish hooks out of the bones of dead fishermen or birds. White items were the most revered, but red was also an important colour, and this may have been due to the redness of the Sun before it appears or disappears over the horizon. Since the Sun's light is white during the day, it is always one of these two colours. The god of feathers was called Era Nuku and feathers were placed to keep away challenging spirits and bring good luck.

How will Makemake help us in the 21st century?

Eastern spiritual beliefs

When Mike Brown made the courageous decision to break away from the century old tradition of naming newly discovered planets after Greek and Roman gods he did something very special for the human race. He made the west turn to look to the east.

In Eastern shamanic beliefs all natural things on Earth are imbued with a magical power, force and energy. This concept has been alien to the west during the reign of Christianity, which worships just a single god. In Christianity we lost our relationship with the environment. Christian missionaries spent years trying to stamp out ancient sacred feminine traditions, which all had deep connections with the environment and natural rhythms. But now quantum science is telling us that sub atomic particles are indeed made of a magical force or energy. They are not just inert, lifeless, solid elements. The Easter Islanders knew this and they totally lived this spiritual understanding.

The unique and special skills required to blend with the celestial stars and paddle according to their movement, or blend with the ocean's currents and understand instinctively what they mean, signifies a very special relationship with nature which we will probably never be privileged enough to know.

The people in this quadrant also understood the presence of the other dimensions, the existence of which is now accepted by modern scientists. They understood different planes or dimensions, where souls and spirit exist as pure energy. Spirit could be communicated with through ancestors who were nearer to the deity because they had passed over. To the Islanders, the other realm was an ever present reality and they were always in dialogue with it. When the first contact was made, the island chief was seen to be constantly talking to either his guardian spirit or Makemake. In 1955, Thor Heyerdahl wrote that the island mayor was always consulting with his spiritual guides and he would talk to them, then pause and listen. When the mayor's granddaughter died in an accident he was comforted by the knowledge that she could now help the family from the 'other side'.

The fundamentals of all these eastern spiritual beliefs will become known and important to us in the future. There is a huge shift in our spiritual consciousness taking place, and it is a move towards eastern or Polynesian spirituality.

Our exploration of the Cosmos and a gung-ho, seafaring spirit

Whilst Makemake has a gentler, submissive, water side, he also represents the spiritual element of fire, and supported a race with competitive, fearless confidence and strong connections to the realm of spiritual support. It is this pioneering spirit that first put mankind in an aircraft and then a space rocket, or in this case an ocean-going canoe to sail for thousands of miles.

That journey exists for us again now. As a human race we are reaching out with all the curiosity of those early Polynesian explorers, expanding and crossing new horizons at a rapid rate. So we will need the same gut instinct and trust that the Cosmos, the god-ness, the ancestors and Mother Nature gave to the Polynesian scouts and pioneers. Early astrological indications seem to suggest that Makemake represents piracy, which could be seen as an audacious practice requiring skillful seamanship.

The theme of duality occurs throughout all Kuiper Belt planets

It is interesting to see this concept reinforced again by the appearance of a dwarf planet in our Solar System whose meaning resonates with it. The story of Makemake's home, Easter Island, includes many dual realities. This contrast was echoed in the population, who occupied two distinct halves of the Island. The Island straddles the edge of the Polynesian empire, and the New World empire. The Islanders lived at the centre of two worlds. The Spanish and New World civilisation was stretching west and the spread of civilisation from China and the Far East was spreading east. Easter Island was therefore, true to its ancient name as the navel or centre of the world.

In the 20th century, when the Islanders embraced Christianity and their dearly beloved minister Sebastian Englert, they led two spiritual existences with two religions. By day they prayed and sang in the island church and by night a dark and secret world of spirits, demons, ancient taboos, human skeletons and secret caves sprang into life. Charms, superstitions and sorcery were all part of their life. Christianity was a thing apart and they easily handled both. There is a surface level to life, and an underground cave level to life and one underlies the other. The Islanders easily absorbed and exaggerated the dual nature of their lives. Their other dimension was the realm of ancestral spirits who communicated with them and could help or hinder.

All this can be seen as a metaphor for the dimension that we live in and the unseen 'dark' or invisible dimension that science has now proved to intertwine with ours. Makemake is the spirit that abides in this other realm, but can be called upon to assist in this one. The Islanders acceptance of both worlds fitted well with general Polynesian beliefs, where the other dimension exists in all things in our realm.

The concept of duality could be found in the issues that the ancient Peruvians had about twin births. One was acceptable but the second was regarded as trouble. One was light and one was dark. It could represent an unconscious part of us that seems to work against us at times because it has a different agenda and therefore might be termed as 'trouble'.

Rabbits and more rabbits!

Whenever I look at the drawings of the 'birdmen' I can't help seeing rabbits! What everyone else sees as a beak, I see as rabbit's ears, and the body shape is more like a dead rabbit on its side than a bird! Go back and look at the illustrations again. Can you see a rabbit? Records say that rabbits had to be introduced to Easter Island; they are not indigenous, so a rabbit symbol makes no sense at all. The only connection with rabbits is the nickname that the astronomer initially gave the planet – Easterbunny. And yet an astrologer's instinct still says rabbits! Also, the Islanders had at some stage built houses that were deeply embedded in the earth like burrows and only had small entrances.

Maybe the rabbit feeling has something to do with the legendary sexual activity and fertility of rabbits or the mythical transformative and magical powers. Legend and folklore always connect rabbits and hares with renewal, fertility and re-birth and this is completely in accord with the sexual proclivity of the Islanders and their beloved Makemake.

Makemake brings abundance. Illusion or not?

When Admiral Roggeveen landed for the first time in 1722 he wrote in his official log that "The island was found to be destitute of trees, but with a fertile soil producing bananas, potatoes, and sugar cane of extraordinary thickness." He is also reported as saying "singular poverty and barrenness". Who is right? There are many other such references to the abundance on the island, for instance: "and a soil which with very little labour furnished excellent provisions"[53] It is possible that the Islanders habit of saying what the person in front of them wanted to hear, also stretched to the island itself. The visitors saw what they expected to see. If they had an expectation of barrenness, that's what they got. There is something of an illusional quality about the energy. Things looked plain on the outside, but underneath there is mystery. Was there abundance or not? This energy may represent 'The Secret'. The esoteric spiritual knowledge that if you want something you have to truly believe and expect it and then it will become. You can constellate or magnetise it into your life.

Another explanation for the Islander's ability to feed so many on relatively little land may have been their expert management of the land in full harmony with nature and natural law, or, once again, back to Rapamycin which may have worked on the land too. Whatever the reason, they produced far more per acre than we do now.

Comparison of the microcosm of Easter Island to the macrocosm of planet Earth. Over population and depopulation

William Thomson wrote in his report that:

> "The traditions assert that the island was in former ages densely populated, and the legends are supported by the gigantic works

of the image and platform builders... there is every reason to believe that the people were numerous enough to severely tax for their support the limited area of ground available for cultivation."[54]

The Islanders lived in harmony and accord with nature, in mysterious dialogue with earth, animals and sea creatures and perhaps we would regard how they grew crops and fed themselves as miraculous.

However, present day ecology alarm bell ringers have used the Easter Island story as a warning of what could happen to our planet and it is hard not to think along those lines when one reads all the so-called 'expert' books on the subject. Some speculate about what may have happened to the Island's ecology before the arrival of European contact, something that science shouldn't really do! Some of it may be valid, but there were reports that were not really fair. For instance, in 1886, after the Islanders had been reduced to a population of 111, the Europeans landed large numbers of horses, cattle and sheep on the island which were allowed to roam freely, eating their way across the whole island. By the mid 1950s the sheep had eaten through so much of the flora, there were only 47 varieties of plant life left! A later scientist then used this fact to claim that the early Islanders had decimated their island. However, it may still be the case that even though the loss of biodiversity happened in the 20th century, Makemake remains a warning about how this could become a great challenge to our planet in the years to come.

Since 2004 scientists have slowly been changing their previous ecocide allegations about the Islanders and this is cause for celebration. Perhaps Makemake has returned to help tell the *real* story of the Islanders before the holocaust. However, there is still a lingering belief that the reduction of Easter Island to a barren wasteland could be a warning to us and this may still turn out to be absolutely valid, even if the early Islanders were innocent.

Meanwhile, there are still unanswered questions about overpopulation and depopulation. Thomson found thousands of houses and skeletons on the island. He commented on the mystery of how that many people lived there with no obvious source of fresh water.

In 2009 Makemake's energy was really heightened astrologically for a while and this allowed a glimpse of what this represents. The Optimum Population Trust is an organization that recognises that planet Earth cannot support uncontrolled population growth. It seeks to support voluntary population controls, managing numbers by disease, starvation and lack of resources.

Some scientists speculate that nature has a natural 'feed-back' loop that will kick in and automatically reduce the population of the planet one way or another. They point to the rise and fall of great civilisations and ask if they succumbed to this natural mechanism. If you have ever kept fish in a pond you will know that they regulate themselves in some way. When the optimum population is reached, one or two obligingly die so that the staus quo is maintained.

Since Makemake presided over a massive depopulation of Easter Island, it is likely that he represents these things in the Collective and these issues will become a focus of world attention.

Makemake and pandemics

Linked closely to the depopulation of Easter Island is the rapid spread of infectious diseases, which were brought to the island by the Europeans. Even when Thor Heyerdahl visited it in the 1950s, the arrival of the annual ship from Chile would be marked by an outbreak of influenza, usually resulting in some fatalities. It was apparent in 2009 that Makemake's energy still resonates with the issue of pandemics. Ironically though, on this occasion, the influenza began in the Americas and spread to Europe. In the 1800s it was the other way round.

Planetary energies, or gods and goddesses, can symbolise a surplus or proliferation of whatever it is they represent, or they can symbolise a lack or loss of it. So therefore Makemake can represent an actual pandemic, the threat of one, or the recovery from one. Now you know who to talk to about any of the above!

Has the Great Sea Spirit returned to guide us into proper use of the seas again?

Religious dynasties of the last 2,000 years have taken us away from nature and the belief of a sacred, divine force in all things. We stopped believing that the Universe was a web with all things dependent on it and each other, and all as important. We believed that as humans we were somehow above and separate to the animals, the wind, the sea and the earth. That we did not need to observe and honour the ways of the ancients and their affinity with nature. Makemake's return symbolises a return to his ways.

It was reported that the Islanders imposed their own fishing restrictions, and did not fish for tuna between May and September[55] and I have already mentioned their harmonious relationship with the seabirds. These are just two examples of how they understood their environment.

It is hardly necessary to remind the reader that we have not been so successful in properly harvesting the fish stocks of our oceans and the situation is now serious. However, marine conservationists are now aware of the problem and how it can be solved. We will need to work with nature and the sea, treasuring, their fragile, sacred power. However, the whole issue is subject to international co-operation. Although we can no longer stand in front of the rising Sun on the winter solstice and look at the brightness of the star group of Pleiades, we have Makemake again and maybe he brings another chance for us to learn his ways.

To finish this chapter I must return once more to the words of the crew member who sailed on the recent historic voyage to Easter Island in a re-constructed canoe using only sails, stars and the sea.

"Surrounded by an immense sea and forced to turn inward, we discovered a harmony within ourselves and with the natural world. For all of us, this voyage had been a rare gift of mana."

These are touching words. We must listen to Makemake again.

"…the traveler… is struck by the solemnity and picturesque beauty of the scene, and is led to ponder on the strange law of progress, which looks so like retrogression, and which in so many distant parts of the world has exterminated or driven out a highly artistic and constructive race, to make room for one which, as far as we can judge is very far its inferior."

William Thomson, paymaster of the USS Mohican, 1891

(**7**)

HAUMEA, HAWIIAN GODDESS OF CREATION, BIRTH AND NATURE

17 *The beautiful land of Hawaii that is Haumea*

Haumea the dwarf planet and the dispute in which two men claimed her

The circumstances surrounding the discovery of a planet tell us a lot about the meaning of that planet in astrology and the meaning of the planet Haumea was obvious right from the beginning of her emergence into the Collective consciousness of the 21st century. The planet Haumea announced herself with the brightest of light and a discovery story involving two groups of astronomers, both claiming her as their own and thus revealing some of her meaning

Haumea the planet was discovered by astronomer Mike Brown around Christmas of 2004. He gave her the nickname 'Santa' and began making the necessary detailed observations. He should really have announced her to the world in July 2005, but he had to take paternity leave at that point.

In July 2005 a team of Spanish astronomers led by Jose-Luis Ortiz also claimed discovery of Haumea. They were examining data collected in 2003 when they had their 'eureka' moment, but unlike the Mike Brown team, they made some enquiries and quickly registered their claim with the official committee. This meant the discovery was technically theirs. Unfortunately their enquiries had led them to access the publicly available weblogs of the Mike Brown team. Mike accused them of stealing his data, which was hotly denied by the Ortiz team.

Because the official naming department couldn't come to an agreement, they decided to say that Haumea had been discovered in Spain but declined to name an official discoverer. So no one man could claim her as his own. Both the American and the Spanish teams had suggested names for her, but the Spanish choice had to be discounted because they had chosen a Spanish Underworld goddess and these names could only be linked to a different part of the Solar System. The naming department must have been relieved because this meant they could use the American name. The man in charge of this committee said the controversy was the worst in 400 years.[1] He also expressed amazement that Haumea hadn't been found before[2] and this is where I say it was always going to happen like this because the Divine works in mysterious ways. Haumea was so bright she could be seen with even a junior telescope. Why is it that all those astronomers over the centuries didn't spot her and then two of them discover her at the same time? It is strange how planets can't be seen until the time is right and then they emerge to tell us something about coming change on planet Earth. Haumea chose the circumstances and the year of her discovery, Mike Brown and Jose-Luiz Ortiz were simply pawns in her game.

Why the name Haumea was chosen

Haumea has two moons that were discovered in 2005 using a large telescope on Hawaii and it was during this time that the name was chosen by David Rabinowitz of the American team.[3] The planet was known to be made of solid rock and the Hawaiian goddess of that name has close associations with stone. It was also recognised that the planet had been hit by objects that had knocked lumps of rocky ice from her body. These are in orbit around her and two of them are even large enough to be moons. In Hawaiian myth Haumea is the mother of many other deities that are formed from pieces of her body.

Haumea is also the Hawaiian goddess of childbirth and Mike Brown was prevented from announcing Haumea's discovery because his wife had gone into labour. These things by themselves make the choice of name appropriate, but there was significantly much more to come!

President Obama and a Hawaiian planet

When the suggestion was put forward for the name Haumea, no one could have dreamed that two years later, just as the name was finally being announced, a young mixed race senator would run for the office of President of the United States of America and win. President Barack Obama was born in Hawaii. Astrology needed to symbolise the changes that happen when the world's most important superpower changes its leader, so sure enough the strange hand of fate worked its magic. Synchronous with the arrival of a Hawaiian born president was the arrival of a Hawaiian planet!

Peculiar features of the planet

Haumea is the strangest object found to date in the Solar System. She is shaped like a cigar and actually spins end over end, completing a full circuit in just four hours. Another strange feature is a red spot on her icy surface.[4]

In 2008 scientists were reporting that they had found eight parts of the planet scattered around the Kuiper Belt. These are remarkable because they are so shiny. This is even more remarkable when we consider that there are eight main islands of Hawaii, and in myth Haumea produces eight offspring which are formed out of her own body.

Haumea, the goddess of Hawaiian mythology

Haumea has several different guises, all to do with creating or giving birth. In one she is a human, confusingly called 'Papa' and married to a man called Wakea. She is thought to be the first woman on Hawaii and therefore the original mother and ancestor of the royal family who always interbred to maintain their pure bloodline. According to Beckworth, she is also the feminine principle or goddess who created the islands of Hawaii. The eight islands are all volcanoes that run along a fault line, some of which still active. When they erupt, the lava spews out, then cools and is added to the landmass. The fire within the volcano is Haumea in her fire goddess form called Pele.

The old Hawaiians have watched the process of land being formed from volcanoes and it has provided them with a wonderful model for understanding how the Earth was created. They equate the fire with Spirit, which is exactly right in spiritual terms, and see that Earth is formed out of fire. The island elders said that the islands rose up as the body of Spirit. They were the material form of spiritual force, and this means that land has an animate nature.[5]

Hawaiian creation chant

The Hawaiians did not record their history in writing, it was told in chants which were learnt more seriously than the western world learns its nursery rhymes. They had an important one called the Creation Chant, which has many different versions throughout the eight main islands. One striking feature is how well they all describe evolution from slime and tiny sea creatures through to larger marine life and mammals. A translation by the last Hawaiian Queen in 1897 says, "Curious students will notice in this chant analogies between its accounts of the creation and that given by modern science or sacred scripture."[6] She also made the point that "The ancient Hawaiians were astronomers, and the terms used appertained to the heavens, the stars, terrestrial science, and the gods." The chant is very long but basically says that the primordial soup was readied and then came 'Time' which supported the Earth and held the Heavens. There is much reference to yin (feminine) and yang (masculine) energies producing all manner of living things and the deities or spirits which pre-exist mankind and are brought into being in their earthly guises, such as surf, octopuses, strife, boils and deep holes. The Hawaiians believe that sacred spirit or deity exists in all things.

Haumea is called different names, from Lailai to Papa, showing that she can take on many different guises; changing from old woman to young girl and becoming her own daughter or granddaughter. We are told that as Haumea, she is great and fearless and has eight different forms ranging from a shark to a goddess or spirit and a human female. Haumea gives birth to children from her brain, amidst slime, and they go on to become chiefs, islands or human babies. So to put it in a nutshell she is Mother Nature transformed into anything. Hawaiian mythology has long lists of things that are either yin or yang.

Haumea as goddess of fertility in wild plants and the forest

In one particular island myth we are told that Haumea's priestesses were privileged to be given a supply of wild food when famine befell the rest of the land. The implication here is that if we are sufficiently knowledgeable about the food that nature naturally supplies then we will be able to eat when mass-produced agriculture fails. In another myth Haumea is killed when a net is thrown over her, and this same net, used during a Makahiki festival, shakes food over the land to encourage good crops. The meaning being that wild food and plants are killed to grow farmed foods. The man who throws the net over Haumea is called Kaulu, whose name means 'growth in plants'. Myth says that he withdraws crops from the land and for some reason this forces Haumea to produce wild food because the soil will not just remain barren; one of gods or goddesses has to provide. Apparently Haumea had wanted to vent her anger by withholding her wild food but it must be provided when cultivated crops are not available at certain times of the year. This shows that although Haumea is destroyer and guardian of wild growth she can be killed by being 'netted' or controlled and will have to succumb to certain conditions.[7]

However Haumea's myths aren't always about wild food. In some she possesses a magic stick called Makalei that attracts seafood and associated with a tree of never-ending food supply.[8]

Haumea as goddess of childbirth and fire

The Hawaiians were told through myth that Haumea could secure a painless childbirth. She was also talked of in the *Hawaiian Book of Medicine* as being able to prevent a Caesarean birth, and would use chants, incantations and herbal medicine to procure a natural birth. Haumea herself was continually growing old and then being re-born and this could describe the process whereby the volcanic islands of the Pacific are born, sink into the sea and then rise up again. As the volcanoes gave birth so easily, so Haumea could make this happen for humans. Haumea was the whole world to them in one form or another and in fact, all the myths describe Haumea as being and doing everything that their island home does.

Several myths refer to her as the goddess of underground heat. This alludes to the red heat inside the Earth that spills from the volcanoes and the also the contents of the uterus. It is said that the fire goddess Pele was born from between Haumea's thighs and other members of the Pele family were born from parts of Haumea's body. Pele was the goddess who lived in volcanoes and sent floods of lava to burn everything. She was said to influence those whose lives were filled with burning anger against their fellow men. Pele was in constant combat with one of her sisters, the ocean. Another sister, Hi'iaka, was a cherished favourite and born in the shape of an egg.

The layers of the Multiverse compared to Hawaiian culture

Hawaiian culture and history is deeply suggestive of hierarchy and 'layers' of significance. Their verbal mythology, handed down from clan chief to clan chief in the form of sacred chants, contains long lists of who begat who, with emphasis on sacred incestuous lineage. They had a heavily demarcated class system of servant families, commoners, upper class and royalty. They had a sacred creation chant that talked of clearly defined 'eras' and their spiritual understanding of the other realms included dimensions of sky gods, earthly spirits and mischief makers, household gods, the home of the spirits of the ancestors and finally the Underworld. Haumea herself had several rebirths, reappearing as her own daughter and then granddaughter and each time marrying her son-in-law and grandson-in-law.

What does Haumea represent in the 21st century?

Haumea, like Ceres, has associations with nature, agriculture and childbirth, but she is very much more involved with creation. There are also some early associations with evolution such as baby dinosaur skeletons. She may well be another representative of Mother Nature's ultimate and omnipotent control over this planet and certainly we get a sense of her independence. Her synchronicity with the arrival of a Hawaiian mixed race president is interesting and maybe like Makemake she will represent under-represented or indigenous races. Certainly she will share involvement with a new Collective spiritual awareness since she epitomises the belief that divine spirit is within nature and all matter is imbued with magical force and energy.

Haumea rules natural cycles such as those of the Moon

The Hawaiian indigenous people worshipped the Moon and the lunar cycle was of paramount importance for planting and harvesting. Each day of the cycle had a different meaning with associated instructions and this was ruled over by the aristocracy and the sacred laws of taboo. Each Hawaiian knew exactly where the Moon was on that day and just what that meant. According to Clive Ruggles, the importance placed on the position of the Moon in agriculture is still relevant today.[9]

The Moon's gravity is so strong that as it passes over the surface of the Earth all the water in the oceans are pulled towards it. Even the Earth's crust and core is pulled out of alignment by 5 per cent as the Moon passes overhead on her journey around us. This cycle and rhythm is fundamental to our existence and spiritual well-being and yet we have all tuned it out and tuned in to street lamps, microwaves and mobile phone masts. Hopefully, Haumea's arrival will mean that the old Hawaiian ways are going to be important in the coming century and we will learn to live that way again.

In the Hawaiian chant we are told that her fabled husband Wakea, became 'false' to her and out of jealousy tried to disrupt the natural rhythms she had established by moving the Moon's days around and using taboo to stop her crossing her threshold.[10] This is a apt metaphor for how humans and science try to control Mother Nature. However, just as her discovery by two astronomy teams at the same time meant that none could claim her, so the human race may find that they cannot claim, own or control her either.

Circadian rhythms and breast cancer

Scientific research,[11] published in 2009, supported the theory that unnatural light at unnatural times causes various forms of cancer. Haumea's natural rhythms of night and day, darkness and light are severely disrupted by the 24 hour working of industrialised nations. Especially at risk are female night workers, who are exposed to a greater risk of breast cancer. This alarming fact is even more astonishing when comparisons are made with blind female night workers, who are getting *less* breast cancer. Apparently, breast tumours are awake during the daylight hours, but rest during the night because the melatonin produced by the body in the dark puts them to sleep. This inactive period dulls the disease because the human, nocturnal, circadian, melatonin signal inhibits human breast cancer growth. Circadian rhythms are physical, mental and behavioural changes that occur in living things and follow a 24 hour cycle, responding primarily to light and darkness in the environment. Apparently, there are abnormally low cancer rates in regions where there is no light for economic reasons. Perhaps candle light would be more appropriate than white strip lights which seem to do most damage.

In astrology there is an association between the Moon and the breasts, so this is a very interesting in the light of the myth regarding Haumea's fabled husband and his meddling with her natural rhythms.

Hawaiian spiritual concept has now been proven scientifically

As I have stated several times already, science has now proved that all matter is made up of energetic force whirling so fast it seems solid. This force pervades and exists in all things giving them dynamic life or energy. It is mysterious and they call it 'dark'. In spiritual understanding this energetic force is that of the element of Fire. This element holds spirit, deity, and what we understand to be gods and goddesses or the Holy Spirit.

The Hawaiians have always expressed this belief through their mythology and the way they lived their lives. They had absolute, unquestioning conviction and faith in this as the meaning of life. In the same way that their volcanic islands arose out of the sea from the fire at the centre of the Earth, the material body is formed out of 'spirit' or energy.

This has to be why Haumea has emerged into world consciousness. Her astrological meaning points out the synchronicity between Polynesian spiritual beliefs and the new understanding of fundamental existence that science is rapidly achieving.

"Behind the (Papa and Wakea legend) is the Polynesian mythical conception of a dark formless spirit world presided over by the female element, and a world of form born out of the spirit world and to which it again returns, made visible and active in this human life through light as the impregnating male element."[12]

That single sentence is actually breathtaking in its accuracy of the new world scientific and spiritual vision of 2008. However, it was written in 1940!

Haumea as nature and sacred earth

It is difficult for us in western culture to even begin to understand the Hawaiian spiritual concept. And yet it more accurately reflects the true composition and nature of life on Earth and in the Cosmos than our monotheist (one god) separatist culture does.

An Hawaiian cultural historian says this:

"Hawaiian culture evolved in close partnership with its natural environment. Thus it does not have a clear dividing line of where culture ends and nature begins. In a traditional Hawaiian context, nature and culture are one and the same, there is no division between the two."[13]

They had such a healthy relationship with their land and nature that both flourished. In the west we are either poisoning our land, or piling concrete on it. We intensively rear chickens so that thousands are crammed into appalling conditions with no space or light. They are so weak they cannot even stand up and they have no feathers due to stress and crouching in their own excreta. Supermarkets proudly sell their bodies for a pound or two.

We don't understand that what we do to chickens and our land affects our spiritual well-being because we are all part of the same Universal spirit or force; it is part of us and it exists in all things. The force, energy and spirit of Mother Nature or Haumea *is* the landscape and it is also us. I think this is something we will all have to learn one way or another.

"Behind (the Haumea legend) is a Polynesian mythical conception of a dark formless spirit world presided over by the female element, and a world of form born out of the spirit world and to which it again returns…"

Beckworth, M. Hawaiian Mythology p306 (1940)

8

Eris, Goddess of Strife, Stimulation and Rivalry

18 *The fiery Eris*

After spending the last two chapters in Polynesia and the Pacific Ocean, we now return once more to ancient Greece. But this time, instead of grappling with concepts of separate dimensions and our creation and place in the Multiverse, we are lectured on personal responsibility and the laws of natural justice. Like Ceres, Eris is within our personal grasp and although mighty in her effect, we *can* learn to respect and work with her.

The discovery of Eris, thought to be the tenth planet

Eris is in the Kuiper Belt, the doughnut shaped ring of planets, rocks and icy debris at the very edge of our Solar System. She was discovered along with Haumea, Makemake and Sedna by Mike Brown and his team during a five year survey that took place early in the 21st century. Eris was first photographed in October 2003, but it took them a while to sift through all the photographs, so it wasn't until January 2005 that an ecstatic Mike realised he had a big planet on his hands and unofficially called the planet Xena and her moon Gabrielle. The nickname Xena had been taken from the hit television series called 'Xena the Warrior Princess', and the name Gabrielle from her sidekick in the show.

Eris is actually bigger than Pluto and was therefore entitled to be called the tenth planet, so the discovery was earth shattering. But then came the problems! When two separate teams of astronomers discovered Haumea at a similar time, this started a squabble for ownership. One of Mike's main concerns was that the other Spanish team was calling Haumea the tenth planet, which he knew to be untrue because he had the much bigger Eris up his sleeve. In an effort to make sure that Eris got her rightful recognition, he hastily called a press conference and announced Eris to the world in July 2005. Mike was angry with the Spanish team and described them as "hackers without scruples".[1] Then a row erupted about the term 'planet', and this had to be settled before Eris could be properly named. The international astronomers held a raucous meeting that resulted in making new rules that stopped Eris being named the as tenth planet. These rules meant that Pluto would no longer be called the ninth planet of the Solar System and was demoted to 'dwarf planet' status along with Eris. All this was a lengthy process, so it wasn't until September 2006 that Xena and Gabrielle were finally given the official names of Eris and Dysnomia.

There is an interesting twist here. Dysnomia is the daughter of Eris in myth. Dysnomia is the Greek goddess of lawlessness, and in the show 'Xena the Warrior Princess', the part of Xena is played by Lucy Lawless, her real married name!

Another interesting co-incidence is seen in the horoscope of Lucy Lawless, which features a very strong connection to this planet. It says that the destiny and purpose of her whole life will be firmly bound up with the energies of the planet Xena and Eris. Lucy is quoted as saying that she loves "being as psycho as I can possibly be." (For the astrology buffs Eris conjuncts Sun, Moon, Asc. N.N. and Saturn in Aries in the first house of Lucy's natal chart.)

The write up of the show speaks volumes:

> "In a time of ancient gods, warlords and kings, a mighty
> princess is forged in the heat of battle. Her name is Xena, and
> only her courage and passion can restore order to a world in
> turmoil, a world crying out for a hero!"[2]

Those are extremely comforting words in this day and age. Could Eris really be our hero? The mythology reported by her discoverers is as follows:

> "In Greek mythology, Eris is the goddess of discord and
> strife. She stirs up jealousy and envy, causing fighting and
> anger amongst men. All the gods except Eris were invited to
> a wedding. Enraged at her exclusion, she spitefully caused a
> quarrel among the goddesses that led to the Trojan War."[3]

At first glance, it is hard to see a similarity between these two descriptions but we'll press on!

Although Eris is usually much further out than Pluto, and takes roughly 560 years to go round the Sun, she has an oval shaped orbit and sometimes comes closer to the Sun than Pluto. At the moment she is farthest away, at 97 times the distance between the Sun and the

Earth.[4] She will be at her closest in 2257, at only 38 times the distance. Her brightness is surprising her discoverers though, so even though she is so far away, her influence cannot be ignored. She has been in the Zodiac sign of Aries since her discovery and will not leave this sign until around the middle of the 21st century. You will particularly feel her influence if you are were born on, or shortly after the 9th April.

A religious cult called Discordianism

When the Romans adopted Eris they called her Discordia, and she is often referred to as the goddess of chaos. Strangely, between 1958 and 1959, a cult religion was formed (supposedly in a bowling alley!), which adopted the theme of discord and chaos and called itself Discordianism. Its proponents recognise that disharmony and chaos are valid aspects of reality, and have a real place in the Universe. They offer an alternative to organised religion, which they see as the "opium of the masses". Since the naming of Eris, this group has had an upsurge in popularity, with Amazon selling out of their original books. (This will be astrologers trying to find out what the planet means!)

The mythology of Eris

According to Greek mythology, Eris is the goddess of strife. She is either the sister or the companion of the god of war, Ares. We are told that the Greek Eris is sinister and mean, and her greatest joy is to make trouble. When she was not invited to an important wedding, she turned up with a golden apple with the words "for the fairest" inscribed on it, and tossed this before the group of the most important goddesses. These were Hera, the wife of Zeus, Athena, a warrior goddess and Aphrodite, the goddess of love. The goddesses began quarrelling with one another over who was the most beautiful and they eventually called on Zeus to choose between them. Recognising the trouble that would befall him if he did, he ordered a mortal man called Paris to choose the winner. Paris chose Aphrodite after she promised to make the most beautiful woman in the world fall in love with him. This happened to be Helen of Troy who was already married, and the consequential love affair started the Trojan War.

The *Dictionary of Classical Antiquities*[5] states that Eris is the goddess of discord, fighting and quarrelling. Further information about her tell us that she calls forth war, and according to the *Iliad* she wanders about small and insignificant at first, but she soon raises her head to heaven.

Her other associations in myth

Eris is the daughter of night and mother of gods and goddesses of trouble, toil, oblivion, hunger, pain, murder, carnage, brawls, disputes, ruin, forgetfulness, deceit and finally lawlessness.[6] (Never did a goddess look so attractive!) Here you see how the ancient Greeks, just like the early Polynesians, believed that the deities *were* the feelings and energies of living; the natural responses of human beings and civilisation. The gods were not separate individuals but could be parts of the feelings and responses that we all experience. So we each have the potential to unleash our Eris and then encounter the difficulties that she gave birth to. For instance you could experience the feeling that you have not been acknowledged for something you feel proud of, and this would stir the revengeful Eris in you. Feeling snubbed and humiliated you might then experience brawls, disputes, or any other of the deities that Eris gave birth to. Mythology was used to counsel the population on a simple level and introduce them to the lessons of life.

A goddess who represents the natural law of fire and the chaos of the God-ness

All the religions and sacred texts of the world have a creation myth with an orderly universe being created out of chaos, fire, energy and spirit. This realm is the 96 per cent of the Multiverse and everything in our Universe draws from it. In this quantum realm, particles that make up an atom are very 'excited' vortices of energy that move at light speed and beyond. Eris is a representative of this realm of fire. In myth, she so delights in the tumult of war, she stays on the battlefield rejoicing in the havoc when the other gods have withdrawn. This is Eris's delight; the chaos is exhilarating and she feels elation in the mayhem.

The positive side of Eris in myth

But there is a more positive side to Eris. In the myth, she only caused trouble when she was not being included. Her story seems to say that she is clever and if we exclude her she will find a way to make her energy felt. Her discovery started a quarrel between the world's top astronomers, but it forced them to sort out certain issues that had been ignored for years. Namely, their computer security, 'new planet' protocol and Pluto's true status.

According to the *Dictionary of Classical Antiquities*, "She was the personification of noble rivalry, and is represented as stimulating even dullards to exertion."[7] However, as we shall now see, the Greek writer Hesiod had the greatest insights into the positive aspects of Eris.

Using Hesiod to understand how to engage with Eris energy in the most positive way

Living life to take advantage of Eris's competitiveness

In order for Eris energy to be effective it has to be strong, volatile and vicious. This energy can easily become "slanderous-tongued envy, with look of deadly hate, rejoicing in the misfortunes of others."[8]

However, I have always found that there is a positive side to everything, including misfortune, and Eris is no different. I was therefore pleased to find an excellent dissertation written by a Heber Michel Hayes in 1918 for the University of Chicago, and I refer to it here. It is the examination of a piece of writing by the Greek philosopher Hesiod called "The Works and Days" and written in the 6th to 8th century.[9]

There is a good and bad Eris and the whole energy is essentially about ethics and karma. The bad Eris is "lawless strife" which has no regard for others and is often seen in the animal kingdom, while the good Eris abides by natural justice and is stirred into serious and purposeful action.

In order to get the best out of this powerful goddess, mortals are urged to stop their emotions being swayed by Eris's cruel and spiteful passions. We should also avoid not caring for others, cruel recklessness and wickedness or perversity. But most of all there are two things required of mortals and these are labour and justice. Let's have a look at the labour part first. Perses is urged to stop bad Eris taking him into vengeful acts that will prevent him labouring. Hay's interpretation of Hesiod explains that the good Eris will support the worker who passes another worker in the race for wealth and prosperity. She is a blessing because she gives us a healthy envy of others that will stir us into action when we see their achievements. We look at their wealth and industry and determine to achieve our own success. If we go with the bad Eris then we may get involved in vengeful acts of envy and dishonesty that waste our time and prevent our own success. Hesiod clearly demonstrates the two different faces of Eris and Hays says:

> "They are vividly portrayed, the one impelling to dishonest
> and forcible aggression, the other to honorable and peaceful
> competition. The dramatic opposition of the two is striking."

Hesiod's demonstration of the two different aspects of Eris once again emphasises the theme of duality of the Kuiper Belt planets. Things are never what they seem on the surface.

Good Eris as part of the natural system of justice

Eris gave birth to energy that punishes perjurers, those who don't honour their oaths, and those who lie to win.

We are especially warned against legal trials in an effort to extract that which is not morally ours. Since western culture is entranced with 'no win, no fee' solicitors and loves suing or blaming others for misfortune, then I think Eris's emergence is nicely timed. Solicitors beware!

In an effort to get the right balance we should hang on to and develop our scruples (the god Aidos) and our indignation at wrong doing (the god Nemesis), keeping a healthy balance between the two. Eris has a family who are personifications of human and karmic ethics, many of which can be found in the Polynesian social system of taboo and mana. It is obvious that she is heavily implicated in a divinely instigated and policed moral system of repercussions and encouragement.

Hesiod declared that we can profit from Eris energy by accepting the laws of Zeus and not bribing the judges to win. The Greeks had avenging spirits called the Erinyes who dealt with retributive justice and they were responsible for punishing crimes not within the reach of human justice[10] and satisfying Oath who is born of Eris. Apparently Oath does more damage than any other to mortals when they knowingly swear to a falsehood. We should trust in the divine providence of Zeus, which means trust that the spirit and divinity of the 96 per cent will attend to things and we should not enter into strife by trying to sort it ourselves. (Okay, sounds fine to me!)

Some final thoughts on Eris

Eris energy has a way of making us feel that we have been got at or picked on, and perhaps this is what earned her such a bad reputation in early Greece. Myth tells us that she 'loves increasing the moaning of men', and there is no doubt that Eris can indeed produce some very irritating energy! On the day that you get overheard by the boss as you call him terrible names on the phone... or you get zapped by a speed trap... or your computer gets a virus... you can be sure that Eris is involved. But then, perhaps you should have left the job years ago... or shouldn't have been speeding... or should have updated your virus software! More importantly, it seems, we should not engage in bitterness and vitriol when it appears that life or someone else has gotten the better of us. We have some very encouraging philosophy from Hesiod on her useful aspects and thanks to this we can understand and perhaps trust and follow the good Eris. That is our choice. We can use her energy to labour hard and surpass others with our industry, or we can wallow in spiteful jealousy and moaning.

We are told in myth that she wanders around small and insignificant to start with, but soon raises her head. It is apparent that she is still in the 'small and insignificant' phase, and we haven't really seen the extent of what Eris can do yet. Mike Brown is convinced that she has the power to start another world war, and although he is not an astrologer, he has experienced Eris's very potent energy for himself. However, I would like to go back to the words of the publicity men in Xena, the Warrior Princess:

"A mighty princess is forged in the heat of battle and only her courage and passion can restore order to a world in turmoil, a world crying out for a hero."

Planet Earth is in a mess right now, so maybe we need a goddess who will stir us into serious labour and purposeful action. This could be a good time to invite her to the party... we know what will happen if we don't!

9

SEDNA, AN OUTRAGED ARCTIC GODDESS

19 *Sedna within her sea creatures of the Arctic*

We are nearing the end of our journey of discovery, but not the end of our learning, for that has only just begun. The last leg of our journey takes us to the northernmost lands of planet Earth, to the Inuit or Eskimo people of Greenland and Canada and their proud, underworld sea goddess Sedna.

Sedna, a strange new 'planet'

Sedna was discovered in 2003 by Mike Brown, Chad Trujillo and David Rabinowitz, the same team that discovered Eris, Haumea and Makemake during the QUEST survey. She was announced to the world in 2004, but the discoverers have yet to decide *what* she is. This strange and unusual object is so alien to us, that scientists were speechless when they found her. Sedna is a huge distance away and there is nothing else like her. Planets near to Earth and the Sun take around a year or two to make one complete circle of the Sun. Sedna has a very strange orbit that takes over 10,500 years to complete.[1] She swings out in a great oval shaped loop which extends right out into space before swinging back in again. No-one knows why she does this, but there is an intriguing theory that it could be because there is something larger out there that we haven't discovered yet and its gravity knocks her off course.[2] The Kuiper Belt just stops dead on its outer edge; it doesn't peter out slowly, so there is speculation that this is because a big planet has gobbled up all the small ones.

When Sedna is furthest away she is 84 *billion* miles from the Sun. Even at her nearest point to us she is still three times further out than Pluto.[3] Our Sun would look so small, that if you were to stand on her surface and hold up a pin, you could hide the Sun behind it.

Half way to the next star there is believed to be a cloud called the Oort Cloud. The theory goes that every so often comets break away from this and travel inwards towards our Sun and there is speculation that Sedna might have come from that cloud. However it is all too far away to be detectable as something has to emit heat or reflect light before our instruments can see it. The stars, for instance, are suns emitting light, so they can be seen. Planets close enough to the Sun can be seen because they reflect the Sun's light and heat. But rocks or planets that are too far from our Sun to reflect the light cannot be picked up. Sedna was just close enough and just shiny enough to reflect a tiny amount of our Sun's light, but the Oort Cloud, if it exists, is even further out than Sedna. It is estimated that her surface temperature is a chilly minus 400°F and this prompted Mike Brown to pick a goddess from the indigenous population of the Arctic Circle for her name.

It was quickly recognised that we would need an expanding vocabulary of classifications or labels, so we would know what to call these new space objects, so the world's astronomers got together in August 2006 and after much debate came up with the term... 'Object'. Or rather an Inner Oort Cloud Object to give her full title. But that doesn't seem appropriate for such a special entity and some astronomers are calling her a 'planetoid'. I am including her in a book about dwarf planets mainly because she was discovered in the same survey by the same team and so has as much to say about our future as the rest of the dwarf planets. However, the description of dwarf planet is technically wrong. Just to make it easy I'm going to use the term 'planetoid' because I think she deserves some status, and she doesn't seem to be the kind of goddess we should sniff at, as you will see!

As with Pluto, size definitely does not count. Sedna is about half the size of our Moon, and yet she has been powerful enough to cause all kinds of weather events here on Earth.

The myth of Sedna

The planetoid Sedna is named after a goddess of the Inuit or Eskimo tribes who live in northern Canada and Greenland. Her discoverers compared her isolation in the cold, distant reaches of our Solar System with the bottom of the sea in the the Arctic.[4] As they usually picked the names of Greek or Roman deities, this was an unusual departure from normal practice. But Sedna had broken all the rules of the Solar System model with her very existence, so why not break a few more? And that choice of name has turned out to be stunningly appropriate. After only a few years of observation, Sedna the planetoid is clearly representing the themes of her myth, and astrological prediction involving her is not difficult. The worldwide storms and floods of 2006 to 2008 were easy to predict, for instance.

Myths are stories that demonstrate the issues that are important for that culture. Northern Canada and Greenland are vast areas and their cultural, environmental and survival needs alter according to their local issues. This probably explains why there are so many different versions of Sedna's myth. This particular one was published by the anthropologist Franz Boas in 1888.[5]

Sedna was raised by her father and grew up to be very beautiful. Many suitors came to ask for her hand in marriage, but she was proud and considered none of them good enough. Then one day a bird called a fulmar (related to the albatross) arrived and coaxed Sedna with an offer she couldn't refuse. "Come into the land of the birds, where there is never hunger, where my tent is made of the most beautiful skins. You shall rest on soft bearskins. My fellows, the fulmars, shall bring you all your heart may desire; their feathers shall clothe you; your lamp shall always be filled with oil, your pot with meat." Suitably impressed, Sedna agreed, and they set out on the long journey to his homeland. Sedna then discovered that her new husband had lied and her new home was a cold hard rock, with a few fish skins and feathers. Her bed was hard and she had to live on raw fish, which the birds brought her. The myth makes the point that her pride had made her reject the Inuit youth. She cried in the wind to her father, saying that the birds treated her unkindly and she felt like a stranger and wanted to return home. Her father, on hearing of her plight, agreed to take her home. He killed the fulmar, and set off home with Sedna in his boat. When the other fulmars found their companion dead and his wife gone, they flew after them. (The story goes that they were very sad over the death of their poor murdered comrade and this explains their mournful cries to this day.)

They found Sedna and her father and stirred up a raging storm. The sea rose in immense waves that threatened the pair with destruction. Fearing for his life, the father offered Sedna to the birds by flinging her overboard, but she clung to the edge of the boat. The cruel father then took out a knife and cut off the first joints of her fingers. Falling into the sea they were transformed into whales, the nails turning into whalebone. Sedna still clung to the boat, so he cut off her second finger joints, which swam away as seals, and when the father finally cut off the stumps of the fingers they became ground seals.

This version reports that Sedna was finally allowed back into the boat by her father, but life was still very unpleasant after that. Other versions say that after her father cut off her fingers, she sank to the bottom of the ocean and became the supreme underworld goddess.

There are some wildly different stories, but her early refusal to marry seems consistent. The Inuits seem to make the point that she didn't come from them, and she wouldn't marry into them. Another consistent story line throughout all the different myths is that her fingers are cut off, and these become sea creatures.

This myth is a wonderful metaphor for Man, the patriarchal or masculine, versus Mother Nature, the matriarchal or feminine. It shows how man has treated Mother Nature. How we have abused her for our own ends and how she has tried to be creative even when repeatedly attacked. For instance, when her fingers were cut off she turned them into beautiful seals and walruses. The myth explains the outrage and fury that Sedna now turns on Man and the patriarchal. It explains in simple terms how Man will strive to control Mother Nature but how she will always win in the end.

Sedna, the Inuit and the shaman

Sedna is the most important and dominant of Inuit deities. She rules the underworld, a place called Adlivun, and from there she controls the climatic conditions and the supply of seafood.

As Goddess of the Oceans, Sedna applies strict rules and conditions for the Inuit to fish by, or she withholds the seas bounty until properly appeased. One of these rules is with regard to the animal as it is killed. The hunter must not damage[6] or injure the animal and leave it in pain, he must kill it properly. If any rule is broken, the tribe's shaman leader, (called an angekkok) has to appease her by making a spiritual or shamanic journey to visit her in the Inuit underworld.

This introduces us to the concept of the shaman and shamanic practise, which may be on the rise in western spiritual circles. The angekkok will face a series of obstacles as he makes his way down to Adlivun,[7] the kingdom of Sedna. He may meet a dog (some myths say her husband was a dog, not a fulmar) or Sedna's father who will attempt to attack the shaman. When he finally reaches Sedna he must comb her hair as an act of humbleness and reverence while he finds out what the tribe must put right before they starve. She doesn't have fingers to comb her own hair and apparently the evil deeds of humans are like dirt in her hair, so the shaman has to comb them out. The manner in which the angekkok engages with Sedna exposes one of the effects that Sedna can have on people; he can either be aggressive and violent, or submissive and serving. He may even repeat the process of cutting off her fingers to release the sea creatures that will feed the human population.

Inuit shamans have spiritual powers that enable them to pass into a state of trance. They can be taken over by spirits and scream and struggle in seizure. They may also speak in ancient dialects or be physically sick. On emerging from the trance they will tell of future weather conditions and expected fishing or hunting success.

Primal force of nature and stroppy redhead

Sedna is believed to be one of the primal forces of nature by the Inuit people. She is both deeply feared and deeply respected. From her position as Goddess of the Sea, Sedna now has ultimate power over the survival of the whole Inuit race, and appears to be demanding and awkward with it. The Inuits also have a Moon-god who has powers over water but he is less ferocious. After first being abused by the males in her life, Sedna becomes powerful and abusive back. Her fury can be seen in the power of the storms she sends, which will now make Man pay homage to her, as in the act of the shaman combing her hair. This tells of her vanity and her pride, but also points to her wounding at the hands of the patriarchy and how she must be tended to as a result of her wound. She demands this act of subservience as repayment.

It is interesting that Sedna the planetoid has a reddish tinge to her light, which puzzles the scientists. In the myth Sedna was initially renowned for her pride and her refusal to submit to several suitors. It seems she has the character of the archetypal redhead, although her hair is said to be black.

Animals and humans are interchangeable

The story mixes together human and animal figures. Their beliefs support the common esoteric principle that we are all one energy or unity but with different forces of nature to keep in balance. Sedna is seen as a creative and destructive all pervading presence.

In 'The Animal and the Human', Malcolm Kenton says this:

> "A central aspect of the religious traditions of several Eskimo tribes... is the existence of the Sea Mother, who is both as a real creature living on the ocean floor and a spirit residing within sea creatures (as well as land creatures, according to some tribes)...
>
> Since the Eskimos depend on sea creatures for most of their food supply, keeping the Sea Mother happy is an important aspect of their endeavours. She is seen as having control of the souls of many creatures, which are able to take either animal or human form, and as a union of opposites. Her power is respected as greater than the human because people are utterly dependent on other creatures for survival."[8]

What does Sedna mean now?

Naming a planetoid after Sedna signifies an enormous awakening of her energy and meaning in the Collective. This boosts the divine feminine energy in the Cosmos with a prominent and controlling symbol of outrage, pride and nobility, but Sedna also has some other specific associations. As with all the planets or deities, they can symbolise abundance *or* depletion of these associations. For instance, Sedna represents the frozen polar regions and in the early 21st century these are disappearing fast. She rules the weather conditions that make or melt the ice by controlling such things as the jet stream and massive undersea currents. She also represents animals that depend on these conditions, such as polar bears, who are facing extinction as their hunting grounds disappear. On the other hand there has been a worldwide increase in storms and consequential flooding, which also comes under her influence. If you remember, the shaman would predict the weather after visiting Sedna.

History of global warming and retreating ice in the polar regions

Around 12,000BC the Earth began to thaw after the last Ice Age and the glaciers covering the northern hemisphere began retreating. It is estimated that there may have been a global population of around four million by 10,000 BC, as opposed to over six *billion* now.[9] They were stone age hunter-gatherers who made jewellery, pottery, statues and hunting tools and we know that they enjoyed cave art, oil lamps and honey. But as the Ice Age was ending there were some strange global phenomena, which the scientists of today puzzle about. The gradual and steady warming was inexplicably interrupted by sudden, extreme global cooling that spanned many years, a period called the Younger-Dryas.[10] At the University of Michigan they have been researching theories on just what could have happened between 10,000 and 11,000 years ago to cause this sudden cold snap in the otherwise warming global climate. Apparently, during this time the Great Lakes virtually dried up. The university's geologists are examining core samples to provide some evidence. This is essential to "help scientists predict the potential effects of rapid changes produced by different factors, which are currently affecting Earth's climate," says the University of Michigan on its website.[11] Their theory is that the amount of melt water didn't just raise sea levels, it threw the world's weather completely off balance.

Another report from the National Academy of Sciences also discusses these extreme and rapid temperature shifts, but this one goes further by demonstrating not just the sudden drop in temperature, but also a huge leap of up to 16°C in the annual temperatures that followed it.[12]

The report said that these leaps could occur over a mere decade. Confirmation of the information in that report came from another source, which stated that ice core records from Greenland showed a sudden warming of around 15°C in the annual mean temperature.[13]

All I can conclude is that Sedna was in the same part of her cycle that she is in now and there was extreme global cooling and then warming.

Possibly connected to these weather events was another phenomena that occurred around this time period. It seems that at least 35 different species of large mammals in North America were wiped out. These included rhinos, woolly mammoths, the sabre-toothed cat, giant rabbits, horses and camels. In 2002, Dr Grayson,[14] an anthropologist from the University of Washington in Seattle, said that he blamed global climate change or more specifically "rapid warming that triggered wide scale trauma". He was ahead of the game on climate change[15] while his peers were sticking to the theory that man had hunted and killed them into extinction.

Global warming and retreating ice

In 2004, a few days before the announcement of Sedna's discovery, scientists and academics issued frightening predictions of the effects of global warming via a leaked Pentagon defence advisor report:

"Climate change over the next 20 years could result in a

global catastrophe costing millions of lives in wars and natural disasters… a former chief executive of the Meteorological Office likens the threat of climate change to that of terrorism… the planet is carrying a higher population than it can sustain. By 2020 catastrophic shortages of water and energy will become increasingly harder to overcome, plunging the planet into war… the potential ramifications of rapid climate change would create global chaos."[16]

In March of 2006, the US Environmental Protection Agency's own website reported this:

"…new evidence that glaciers draining the ice sheets of Greenland and western Antarctica have recently accelerated. Some have more than doubled their speed over the past five years… rapid increase in glacial quakes during the last four years. Simulations suggest that the climate in Greenland could become as warm by 2100 as it was approx. 130,000 years ago… an eventual sea level rise of as much as 20 feet in the coming centuries. This could proceed at rates of up to three feet per century."[17]

Reports like those above did start to emerge around 2003, but they didn't really get a lot of media attention. By 2006 the whole subject was really taking off and newspapers were reporting on the crisis. The *Independent* newspaper[18] gave the whole of its front page to a photograph of melting polar ice and in a six page article reported that it had shrunk by 14 per cent in just a few months between 2004 and 2005. That was compared to an average of 0.15 per cent per year since records began in 1979. The overall loss amounted to an area the size of Turkey. Although Sedna had been discovered and there is no doubt that this coincided with the massive melt down, it didn't really become the top global issue until

2006. Likewise, in astrology, Sedna started to become really active in that year. The report in the Independent appeared at such a time.

"An Inconvenient Truth" and the International Polar Year Initiative

At crucial times for Sedna astrologically, there were some interesting events that made world news. The first, around May 2006, was a film called 'An Inconvenient Truth' and featured Al Gore. Until then America, led by George Bush, was in denial about global warming. He had withdrawn from the Kyoto Treaty that would have bound America to lowering CO^2 emissions. The next event was the launch of the International Polar Year Initiative, a major scientific programme focusing on the Arctic and Antarctic from March 2007.[19] This programme would be instrumental in getting world governments to pay attention to the crisis of melting ice. It found cataclysmic warming and loss of snowfall. The lack of snow is serious when you consider that usually, 100 billion snow crystals are formed by our planet every *second*.[20] This production rate is necessary to maintain the climate in the colder regions. If it lessens, there are serious repercussions. However, if Sedna was giving less snow to the polar regions, she was certainly increasing precipitation elsewhere. If there is one thing the summers of 2007 and 2008 will be remembered for, it is rain... lots of it!

Sedna the planet could be used to predict storms and floods

From February 2006 until December 2008, Sedna the planet was in a relationship with another planet in the sky that made it easy to correlate weather events with her influence. As certain planetary formations occurred, there was a corresponding weather event here on Earth. In order to discount allegations that one can always find a storm or hurricane resulting in flooding somewhere on the planet, I used a certain rule to measure the validity of this coincidence. If the weather event was reported on Sky news in the news headlines, then it was big enough to be counted as extraordinary and linked with the specific astrological aspect of Sedna. Fortunately the specific astrological aspects are mathematical and precise so can be checked out by any astrologer. There were many correlations and I'll just give a brief summary of them:

'The film entitled 'An Inconvenient Truth' released May 2006
Global warming became hot news, September 2006
International Polar Year Initiative launched, March 2007
World Met Office[21] reported global land surface temperatures highest
 ever and record amounts of rain, January to April 2007
Snow in South Africa, June 2007
Cyclone in Saudi Arabia, June 2007
Floods in England, June and July 2007
Severe floods in India and China, July 2007
Storm left over from Hurricane Joanna hits England, March 2008
American Mid West flooded, March 2008
Floods in Ireland and Scotland, August 2008
Heavy rainfall England, September 2008

As I said before, these events had to be severe enough to make the Sky news headlines. One observation I have made is that Sedna seems to be responsible for the storms, rainfall and winds that cause the eventual flooding, rather than the flooding itself, although it is the flooding that has the greater effect on our lives.

The tsunami of 2004 and the sinking of Atlantis 12,000 years ago

The great storm summoned in her myth and her rulership over ocean life give us signposts to Sedna's meaning, so when the Indian Ocean suffered a massive tsunami in 2004, the year of Sedna's discovery, it was natural to associate the two things. It was certainly a very significant event, it being the biggest tsunami that the world has ever known with an estimated 200,000 killed.[22] According to a BBC report, a sea surge was triggered when an earthquake caused the seabed to rise up, displacing the water above it. This turned into giant shock waves that travelled at speeds of up to 497 miles per hour. It may be too soon, however, to attribute this tsunami to Sedna alone and certainly there are astrological pointers that may implicate Makemake as being the god who resides over tsunamis.

Interestingly, there was remarkably little loss of animal life. Elephants sensed it was coming and stampeded to high ground. Given Sedna's protection over the creatures of the deep, and animals in general, it would be in keeping with her spirit to save them. Many ancient cultures on Earth have a flood myth, so it is reasonable to assume that all of them speak of a huge flood that killed all but a few. But the Bible, at least, speaks of the careful saving of the animal species so they can re-populate and again, this is consistent with Sedna's theme.

In 2005 the BBC[23] reported that a Dr Gutscher had found sediment evidence of a large earthquake and tsunami that would have struck a submerged island in the Straits of Gibraltar around 12,000 years ago. This island, called Spartel Island, had once been above water and has been suggested as the likely candidate for the origin of the Atlantis legend. The Greek philosopher Plato wrote of Atlantis[24] and suggested that it sank in a huge one day event. He took his information from oral accounts that had been handed down over a period of 9,000 years and said this:

"There occurred violent earthquakes and floods. And in a
single day... the island... disappeared in the depths of the sea."

He reported that Atlantis sat off the coast of north west Africa and was inhabited by an advanced civilisation. The interesting connection with Sedna is her cycle around the Sun of 10,500 years, in which she is nearest to the Sun for well over 500 years. Since that estimate may not be exact, or the 12,000 year time span for the sinking of Atlantis may differ by a few thousand years, it may make the two events synchronous. There is certainly enough evidence to at least include it in this chapter, while leaving the final answer to posterity.

Hurricane Katrina

This was also an extraordinary event, which happened in August 2005 and, like the tsunami, it was before the 2006/2008 period of high and consistent Sedna activity. On this occasion the planetoid was receiving energy from Mars, the planet of violent energy, and he may have triggered this opening debut from her. Although Katrina was only the third strongest hurricane in American history, she was the most destructive and deadliest because she hit the town of New Orleans, which is overcrowded and below sea level. When the flood barriers collapsed, the city flooded with 20 feet high water and that killed around 1,800 people.

A quote from a report issued by the United States Environmental Protection agency in 2006 states that "The number of category four and five hurricanes has increased by 80 per cent world wide during the past 35 years, according to a study in the 16/9/2005 issue of *Science* magazine. Hurricanes in these two highest storm categories, with winds of up to 135 miles an hour now account for roughly 35 per cent of all hurricanes, up from around 20 per cent in the 1970s."[25]

They point out that the number of hurricanes hadn't grown, just the intensity of them. This same report has another interesting point. It specifically picks out Louisiana and southern Florida, predicting that over the coming centuries they will "ultimately disappear under the rising seas." Since Hurricane Katrina had a big impact on Louisiana, should we not take it as a warning of the vulnerability of building and re-building cities on land that is already below sea level? Is it not arrogant of Man to think that he can stop the rising sea levels? This is not living within Mother Nature's limits; this is inviting her wrath and scorn. If Sedna was making a point with Hurricane Katrina, it would be unwise not to be more respectful and obedient to what she foretells.

The Great Cycles

As was said previously, planets closest to the Sun take about a year to make one complete orbit around it. The new planets discovered in the Kuiper Belt, on the fringes of the Solar System, take two to three hundred years. Until now, that seemed like an enormous amount of time. Then we discover Sedna and now we are looking at 10,500 years to make one complete orbit of the Sun. This enormous time frame obviously has great significance. We now have to accept that we are part of a *much* bigger cycle,[26] on a much bigger stage. Our horizons have really been pushed out. One of the effects of seeing a much bigger Universe, is to see ourselves as smaller and smaller grains of sand on a beach that just got 10,500 times bigger!

As we try and get our heads around that concept, we can also take into account some other major cycles that occur in our Solar System. Because of a wobble in the Earth's rotation we are in a cycle that is called the Great Cycle or Precession and takes around 26,000 years to complete. Planet Earth doesn't spin perfectly on its axis; it's like a spinning top that whirls round very fast, but also has a slower wobble. A pencil sticking out of the top from the exact middle would draw a circle in the air above the top. This is what the Earth is doing. We don't notice it because it takes about 26,000 years for it to move round in the whole circle. Theoretically, if you sat in exactly the same place every year at the same time and looked through a tiny hole in a wall at a specific star in the sky, it should be in that same place every year of your life. That's because the Earth should have returned to exactly the same place each year. The star never moves, so it should all line up perfectly year after year. However, over the course of 72 years, it will appear to have moved slightly. One degree to be precise. That's one degree out of the 360 that describe the dome of the sky all around you.

However, the star hasn't moved, the Earth has. It may not be much, but over the course of hundreds or thousands of years the night sky changes dramatically because of this wobble. It means that the North Pole points in a different direction during the course of this 26,000 year movement. This in turn changes the direction and angle of the Sun's rays to the Earth and alters average temperatures and planetary conditions accordingly. Particularly at the polar regions, where the Sun can be full on or missing for months on end.

Sedna's long oval cycle around the Sun puts her at different physical locations in different millennia, and so she can accordingly describe different planetary climates.

Cycles are funny things. There are really small ones, like the cycle of electrons whirling round the nucleus of an atom and then there are bigger ones, like the Moon going around the Earth or the Earth going around the Sun. Then there are enormous ones, such as the Earth's wobble, and then even larger ones again. For instance, our Sun is one of 100 million Suns in our Galaxy that spin around a centre and it takes about 225 million years for us to go around the centre once. This is called a Galactic Year.

By contemplating Sedna and her 10,500 year cycle around our Solar System we also contemplate our place and part in these mega-cycles.

Evidence that we have done all this before?

Ancient civilisations knew of this wobble and it is possible that they tried to demonstrate this superior knowledge within the sacred geometry of their buildings. There is much that we still have to discover about this knowledge. They knew papyrus would not survive long and only something as big and indestructible as the Pyramids could survive for many thousands of years. It is a fallacy that 'prehistoric' means lacking in sophistication and intelligence. They may have been far more advanced and developed than we are in ways we don't understand yet.

For all we know, the human race is in a similar 11,000 year cycle to Sedna's. Physically, nothing remains of these ancient civilisations, so how can we prove otherwise? The scientists cannot agree on the accuracy of carbon dating so they could be thousands of years out.

I read an interesting and puzzling report in a journal called *Nature*,[27] two scientists from the Australian National University reported that around 10,000 years ago, fires caused changes in vegetation patterns and produced carbon dioxide emissions that apparently were the cause of global climate change. The pre-historic community "may have been actively engaged in modifying vegetation patterns, regional climate and atmospheric gas concentrations long before the advent of modern concerns over global change. In short, the man-made activity that experts say is causing global warming now may actually be an ancient phenomenon".

Perhaps human civilisation is taken back to near extinction by a flood every 11,000 years, which wipes out all evidence of existing technology. Then we slowly grow to superiority as we have now, then devolve again as weather and planetary conditions deteriorate. Perhaps this is why we believe that civilisation emerged from places like Africa and the Middle East. Because they were least dependent on global support, such as electricity from Norway and water from Scotland. When disaster came they could survive quite well on what they had always had. They had water from their own well and crops from their own land. They won't perish when the seawater rises. The people living in major European cities are more dependent and vulnerable than our primitive cultures.

What can we do?

On a global level

Perhaps Sedna's energy manifests as a yet unidentified huge global underwater current, such as the gulf stream or maybe an air stream such as the jet stream. They discovered a new ocean current as recently as 2009,[28] so clearly they haven't identified all of them yet. Recent scientific theory proposes that the weather anomalies we are experiencing in England may be as a result of the jet stream slackening and kinking which causes unprecedented weather events.[29] For what the ancient indigenous people saw as a goddess, science may name as a physical planetary phenomenon. The Ancients always identified local climate and food sustaining conditions as deity to be respected or worshipped. (As Zeus was recognised as god of thunder in Greece. Once you have experienced how quickly the weather changes and the clouds billow up, then you *truly* understand Zeus's attributes.) However that may be, Sedna still represents Mother Nature and as the Sea Keeper of the oceans her message is that the 'evil deeds' of humans are the terrible pollution and over-fishing that the seas have to bear. We are abusing the world's oceans. Sedna is the symbol of a wake up call from Mother Nature. Each one of us must integrate into our conscious being a sensitivity for our position as "caretaker of humanity and this planet"[30] or we face Sedna's reminders! Let's look at planetary conditions in this latest Sedna awareness time. Is the current "wide scale trauma" now being caused by humans? If so, can we reverse it? According to the International Polar Year report, there is:

"…abundant evidence of changes in snow and ice, reductions in extent and mass of glaciers and ice sheets, reductions in area, timing, and duration of snow cover, and in the extent and thickness of sea ice. Changes in the large ice sheets will impact on global sea levels, affecting coastal cities and low-lying areas. Changes in snowfall and shrinkage of glaciers will affect millions of people… (the thaw) will mobilise vast reserves of frozen carbon, some of which, as methane, will increase the global greenhouse effect. Changes in sea ice combined with enhanced river inputs of freshwater will lead to substantial changes in ocean circulation. Warming of polar oceans, coupled with changes in ice coverage and river run-off, will alter marine ecosystems with consequences for globally-significant fisheries."[31]

Whether or not we caused it, we will have to live with it and make sensible decisions for the future.

On a spiritual level

As I have suggested, it may be time to return to pagan or spiritual beliefs that whole-heartedly embrace the feminine energy and re-awaken our conscious connection to the spiritual plane of existence. This includes connecting to our living, breathing planet; its ethereal relationship to the Sun and the animals. We are not separate from them. For the last 2,000 years, Sedna's message has only been treasured by the esoteric minority and the deeply ethnic cultures, who in the main, do not run the planet. Sedna's sudden thrust into greater prominence symbolically flags up her intention to be heard more clearly now.

Sedna's Inuit people have no organised religion and this may be further evidence that the western world's invasive and restrictive religions are outmoded or in decline. Strict attendance at purpose built mosques and churches for instance, may soon be a thing of the past. The Inuits were and are deeply spiritual, but they have never seen the need to have priests and formal religious structures around them.

I think we connect with Sedna when we seriously, properly and respectfully take care of the planet, and accept Sedna's mysterious omnipresence in matters of the arctic and the weather that springs from its currents. We will have to accept and flow with the cycles we live in from the small one shown us by the Moon, to the large one of precession, but that does not spell our doom. There are very strong fundamental reasons for the long-term success of the human race and I will discuss those in the next chapter.

On a personal level

Those individuals with prominent Sedna energy will have experience of never really feeling completely at home in the sphere of personal relationships. This might range from feeling a little awkward as though something is perhaps 'missing', to an intangible fear of impending annihilation. The ability to feel completely safe might seem strangely elusive for some unknown reason.

It has been suggested that people whose whole lives are influenced by Sedna's energy will demonstrate these themes. In the first part of their lives they may attract aggressive, angry and destructive people to them, then later they may comprehensively spurn and dismiss them.

Sedna types might attract damaged lonely souls who themselves abuse and attack as a wounded animal will. Their task is to move out of this pattern, toughen up and get firm with this damaging cycle.

There are better, more fulfilling things lined up for them than this. They should embrace global issues instead. Sedna types march to a different drum beat. The lonely arctic wastes of an unsatisfactory relationship will eventually present them with no choice. The howling gales will echo round their soul with the voices of a thousand screaming seagulls. They can shrivel up inside from the loneliness and cold around them, or they can spiritually surge into no-nonsense awareness of their own strength and authority. I'm not saying that one-to-one relationships are impossible for them, but they will struggle in the same way as Sedna, until they find a channel for all that cosmic and spiritual power. Then one-to-one relationships can be less stressed and laden with energies that shouldn't be played out in this area. Trying to extract or play out Sedna's powerful authority and familiarity with universal suffering in a relationship doesn't work. If you resonate to an energy that loves and feels for millions of lives, then how do you live this out within the limits of a tiny personal relationship? You can't. The compassion is too immense, the victimisation needs to be too immense, the pain needs to be too immense.

Sedna feels at one with, and has authority over, the whole of creation. As a planet she travels nearly to the next Solar System and back. She feels the pain and loneliness of nearly 11,000 years on her own, and responsibility for the essence or soul of creation. If you have the capacity for that much awareness, it's hard to feel content with the mundane aspects of day to day life.

People who resonate with this should try channeling into animal charities. Become concerned about arctic matters. If you choose to eat animals, which Sedna is not opposed to in the myth, try to eat only those animals that you feel were properly respected.

Become aware that everything is one and you are part of it. Feel your connectedness. Become a caretaker of the planet. The Pagans, Druids and Wiccans have understood this all along. Sedna has come to give this message a focus, and raise awareness globally. The stakes are too high for any one of us to ignore them.

10

" They fought from heaven; the stars in
their courses fought against Sisera…"

The Book of Judges 5:20

WHAT DOES THIS MEAN FOR US IN THE BUS QUEUE?

Looking back over these chapters, it is difficult to get a coherent sense of meaning. Where are we going with all of this? What's going to happen this century? What will happen to our children? Or even 'in the end'?

The doom gloom worst case scenario

Let's look at extreme worst-case scenarios. The very worst things that the arrival of all these new planets and the Kuiper Belt could mean in astrology. (Get a glass of wine first!)

Well, last time Sedna was around, there was rapid climate change and many species became extinct in the extreme temperature fluctuations. Makemake points out that the Easter Islanders initially lived in harmony with nature although they may have had an over-large population. Then the Europeans arrived in the Pacific, causing depopulation through a pandemic of infectious disease and the kidnapping of Islanders. Does this mean 'foreigners' will arrive and kidnap us or wipe out most of us with diseases, or could it mean our ability to feed the world will diminish because we don't live in harmony with nature and the world is over-populated? That's two options.

Option three concerns Ceres. Has she returned to guide us through the Underworld or walk with us in grief? Does her instruction to change the late 20th century attitude to death have a reason behind it? The Egyptian initiates of the Mysteries used to achieve a comatose state and astral travel into higher spiritual awareness before returning to their bodies again. After this they celebrated the 'other side' and feared death no more. Will we come to do the same? Then of course, there's Pluto-Charon. Does his message 'survival of the fittest' and the regulation of souls on each plane of existence remind us that there are too many souls in bodies on our planet? He also promotes the healing power of sex and unlimited, safe, clean nuclear power, so it can't be all bad.

And lastly, why have so many Earth Mother goddesses all appeared at once? Possibly to reinforce seasonal cycles and the care and protection of nature and planet Earth. Think for a moment of how Ceres stopped the rain and dried out all the fields allowing us to bring the harvest home. But, of course, she is also responsible for grief and death rites. Then there is Eris, a strong feminine energy and mighty and maverick defender; ready to intervene with a very heavy hand to ruthlessly maintain universal karma, mana and taboo.

But enough of this doom and gloom! We need to look at the insurances we have against these scenarios, to discover the pot of gold at the end of the rainbow, or the silver lining. But before we do, let's look at the prophecy of an ancient Greek philosopher.

The gold, silver, bronze and iron races

I am referring now to the essay written by Hesiod, called *Works and Days*,[1] first examined in chapter eight. This document gives precise and detailed instruction of how to use the rising and setting of various stars to carry out profitable management of farming and crops.

He urges us to avoid the anger of the deathless deities, which are wise words indeed, but it is his information of the five races that is most important.

First came a race of Gold – the Golden Age – and they lived in perpetual youth without care or toil. After death they became spiritual guardians and givers of wealth here on earth. The second race was Silver and they suffered some woes because they were spoilt and they mollycoddled their children. They had had it too good and they didn't see fit to worship the immortal gods. Since it is essential to honour the blessed deities, Zeus became tired of them. Still, when they died, they did become immortal.

Then, along came the Bronze race, who were strong and terrible. They had brutish, warlike ways and this time they had to suffer the Black Death and go to Tartarus. The fourth race was before our own, nobler and righteous with many heroes who ranked as demi-gods. Their end was in a land of grain-giving earth and sweet flowing honey near an ocean at the ends of the Earth, but still they were untouched by sorrow.

Finally the fifth race, whom Hesiod does not envy. These are the Iron race who toil and work hard. (Recognise anything yet?) Apparently some good men mingle with the evil ones and they die naturally when their hair turns grey. However, children dishonour their parents and chide them with bitter words. It is at this point that envy, bad mouthing and scowling faces will make people feel wretched and no one will look after the elderly. (Any mother of teenagers will be leaning forward at this point!) Respect for justice and oaths will be lost and we will have earned our future, a fate of bitter sorrows with no help against evil.

So now we have that joyous prophecy under our belts, let's continue towards the pot of gold at the end of the rainbow!

Reaching for something bigger or shrinking to smaller

Frontiers are expanding and our view of life has to widen along with our view of the Cosmos. We have to believe in and reach for something 'bigger'. Or do we?

The fears and difficulties of reaching for 'bigger'

Bigger has no meaning if we don't know what to use as a guide. What is bigger? Imagine that you have lived all your life in a small area. It wasn't uncomfortable and you were quite happy with it; but relative to the size of the planet it was infinitesimally small. You developed an understanding of this place and it was all you had to refer to when asked to imagine something else. You couldn't conceive of something bigger because you didn't know what 'bigger' looked like. The only image you could come up with would be a bigger version of the place you already knew. So if your area was in Egypt, then with all the desire in the world your concept of bigger would always be filled with sand and sun. You can't suddenly imagine snow and glaciers just because you are told to 'think bigger'. Likewise, we can't just imagine what bigger is and be accurate.

So now we have a problem. We have to believe in something bigger and have faith in this, but the best thing you can imagine if you have always lived in a desert is an oasis. Things that would help you deal with what you know. You wouldn't know how to dream of ice, not because you can't dream, but because your brain can't imagine ice without already having seen some. So we don't know what to dream of when we are told to think 'bigger'.

Our second problem is fear. We spend our lives overcoming one fear after another. Fear of first going to school, fear of bogeymen and the dark. Fear of losing our parents, fear of not being able to earn enough money and fear of not finding the right relationship. Fear is our greatest motivator. The most potent teacher in our lives is fear. Most of our behaviour will ultimately be as a result of trying to avoid fear. It stands to reason then, that we are not going to be in a rush to take on more fear when we have quite enough for our lifetime, thank you very much.

On the surface of it, thinking of something bigger contains a lot of fear because it involves having to accept that we are not top of the pile and our lives are very insignificant. And if they are insignificant then they could be at risk. Our attachment to them may be threatened and this invokes the fear that we might lose them. Then there is the usual fear of something we don't know or understand. It might harm us. If safety, survival and security are threatened then all the bigger concepts in the world are no substitute. No one with normal human emotions is going to happily substitute their home, children and career for belief in something 'bigger'.

We do not want to see anything that we care about being put at risk for 'bigger' until we can visualise it or see it. Until we've understood it, read about it, tasted it and prodded it we are going to be fearful of it. Until a scientist has put it through rigorous tests and declared it 'safe', it is not to be trusted and certainly no substitute for putting on the blinkers and keeping the small and narrow view. For most people believe that what they can't see won't harm them.

But what if bigger has been there all along? Not revealing itself, just keeping out of sight and out of mind. Okay, we still can't imagine it but at this point we just have to accept that it's there. This is the first stage in a process that will eventually lead to the reduction of fear. First, accept that bigger is there and in this century it will become known to us. As I said, like the Kuiper Belt, it has been there all along. As you have got this far, we can definitely assume that you are willing to believe in something bigger.

So what might 'the bigger picture' be about?

The bigger picture is about accepting in the 21st century that we are just a tiny grain of sand on a beach that is exploding in size. But more than that, all the grains connect to make a giant invisible web. We could see this demonstrated very clearly in the first decade when the financial mistakes of one country suddenly showed themselves to be linked into the much bigger picture of world finances. Suddenly the outstanding loan that Mr Bloggs was unable to pay back on his home in California was impacting on the car worker in Britain who then lost his job.

Leaders of countries became very keen to point out that the financial circumstances of one country could not be isolated from another. A failing bank in Iceland caused big increases in local government taxes in some areas of Britain. This, of course, suited the leaders of countries who could now blame someone else for the gross mismanagement that had happened on their watch. These are examples that demonstrate how things can all be linked into a much bigger picture without us even knowing.

So having accepted that we now have a bigger world to contend with, let us look for the silver lining that will accompany this enlightenment. When looking at our place in a much bigger, spiritual, Multiverse Cosmos, we have to ask what is the meaning of life. What can we believe in that will give us the meaning for our existence and a heaven to work towards? Well just as the world's financial boundaries dissolved and everything got linked up when we weren't looking, so should the world's spiritual beliefs. The previous boundaries and highly segregated religions that have caused such conflict serve no purpose. We need to have a flexible spiritual belief. This should be along the lines of Polynesian belief where all things are imbued with life force and divine energy and 'death' is just the other side of the veil. I hope you didn't miss that last sentence because it is one of the main points of this whole book. We need to adopt the eastern belief that divine life is an energy or force that is present in all things on this planet and we also need to understand that *our* life can exist in many other guises on many other planes of existence. This is what one aspect of bigger means.

Looking at earthly concerns and possible remedies

The population of Earth is becoming unsustainable in its current format, *but*, think back to the Egyptian desert example I used earlier in this chapter, where all we could imagine was a tent and an oasis when asked to dream up a solution. What if we cross the divide between what we can imagine and get to the place where ice and snow are possibilities? Where there is *any* possibility. Okay, it won't be a format we recognise, and we may currently be tempted to dismiss it as science fiction 'rubbish', but maybe the day will come when we can travel to somewhere other than Earth. In any case, Makemake may make sure that the population will only be as big as its ability to grow sufficient local food. (I never liked strawberries in December anyway!)

National industrial growth at all costs may cease to be the Holy Grail of all governments. All global economic growth can achieve is the eventual consumption of all the natural resources of our planet. Nothing left to burn, nothing left to make things out of.

But let's look even bigger and higher still. Let's look at the highest spiritual awareness the dwarf planets can give us and there we will find the answers we seek and the comfort we crave.

The something we have in the 4 per cent that absolutely ensures our future

Before we are born, our soul agrees to be born again. And when we agree to this incarnation, we do it joyously because there is something in the 4 per cent that we can't have in the 96 per cent. And that something is worth all the pain and hardship that we might have to bear now and anything that we might face in the future.

That 'something' is an aspiration and achievement so great, it means the whole of the Multiverse on all planes of existence will co-operate to keep our 4 per cent going.

It is something that we can't have on any other plane. Something that the spirits and angels long for. We know the deities long for it too, because we have so many myths telling us that they lived among mortal men. Why didn't they want to stay on Olympus or transcend into greater bliss and fusion with the Absolute Divine?

This 'something' is the desire for freedom and self-guidance. That bloody-minded, pig-headed need to express oneself as a single, autonomous individual, rather than part of the Divine One-ness in the highest reaches of Multiverse existence. For in the end, many spiritual layers up, there is no individuality at all, not even individual souls, just a spiritual mass of refined energy and perfection.

That said, we do still have some of the aspiration of the higher consciousness of the Multiverse, which seeks out fusion with this absolute spiritual perfection in the highest reaches of cosmic existence. This much we inherit from the divinity of the 96 per cent and the higher Universal Mind; and the whole journey generally seeks achievement through higher and finer grades of existence. But we do find it hard to let go of the self-gratification and self-direction that we enjoy in our Earthly incarnations, down here in the lower levels of existence.

Milton describes this in '*Paradise Lost*'[2] when the Fallen One says:

"Here we may reign secure, and in my choice,
To reign is worth ambition, though in hell!
Better to reign in hell that serve in heaven…"

Helen Blavatsky put it another way in 1888 when she wrote the *Secret Doctrine*.[3] It says:

"Better be man, the crown of terrestrial production and king
over its opus operatum, than be lost among the will-less
spiritual hosts in heaven."

Helen says that fall of man from spiritual being to earthly one is preferable. That he wants this hell on Earth because of:

"that law in nature, which implants in man as well as in every
beast a passionate, inherent, and instinctive desire for freedom
and self-guidance…"

For this reason, because all entities and divinities on all planes want to protect this single possible achievement so much, the 4 per cent and this world will always be protected. It will never be allowed to become non-existent.

Human worship is needed to feed the spirit of the 96 per cent

As I said in chapter three, the gods or spirits depend on our worship and feed off our emotions. Science tells us that dark particles called neutrinos pass through our body at the rate of millions per square centimetre per second. They pour out from our Sun and flood through the Earth some eight minutes later. We know that cell biologists have detected millions of signals passing through the ether in electromagnetic waves to the individual cells of our body where they are decoded and acted on by our nervous system. The passing neutrinos or signals carry with them our emotions. Our love, our passion and our grief. Which is why the love you generate can fill the Universe with its warmth. The deities and spirits need this to exist. And this is why the strongest of all the planets is currently Pluto-Charon whose message and sole (or soul) purpose is to regulate and maintain the existence of the 4 per cent for all the spirit in the Multiverse.

By the way, there is one other reason the gods and godesses want to maintain our plane of existence, which you may remember from the chapter on Ceres. This reason is found in the *Egyptian Book of the Dead* where one god complains to the Great Atum that in the existence beyond the Underworld there is "no drinking, breathing and lovemaking; *only* spirit being and contentment." The deities would rather have these earthly experiences than the bliss of fusion with the absolute perfection of the Universal mind. There is no way that they will allow the demise of our world.

World religion and religious dynasties

So much wickedness has been perpetrated in the name of religion in the last 2,000 years, it is hard not to be scathing about it now. Priests have repeatedly abused young children left in their care. Missionaries have destroyed all the precious spiritual texts and traditions of many civilisations they sought to convert. People who believed in astrology and herbalism were tortured for the sick pleasure of the deeply devout. Crusaders waged terrible wars in order to own and control foreign lands. And although it might be true to say that civilisation itself was relatively barbaric in those days, it is also true to say that many religious dynasties didn't demonstrate much compassion and tolerance.

Makemake and Haumea both symbolise change in religious beliefs. Our spirituality as a human race will move towards eastern concepts such as Buddhism. Or perhaps the major religions will change into something less controlling and structured. Something that dignifies animals and allows for many different gods and goddesses. Something that will allow an individual response to spirituality and not demand it fits into the box and bows down to a humanly controlled hierarchy.

But most of all it is going to have to give us the absolute conviction that peace, serenity and sublime fulfilment are achievable aspirations of the future. Whether that future is in a body or out of it. We want to know that as our loved ones and ourselves depart, we go to a comforting place that holds no fear. Come back pink and fluffy, all is forgiven. Remember, the Egyptian initiates feared death no more. Isis and Ceres showed them higher spiritual consciousness and happiness. They learned that death was not final, that human souls are recycled and take on more life. That there is no death for life. Just as the seed is planted in the Underworld of the dark soil, so the soul goes into the Underworld to be born again. Jesus Christ wasn't the only one to experience resurrection. We all will.

Our religious framework of the future will have to give us this sort of reassurance and comfort. So that we don't fear death, we embrace the potential for moving on and know that we will return. Then our religious and spiritual beliefs can support, calm and reassure us and not fill us with the dread and fear of nothingness or divine retribution.

"The Key" from the Hermetic texts, and the key to it all

To get a good understanding of how our spirit, body and mind are put together, it is illuminating to look at one of the writings from the Hermetic texts.[4] These writings are attributed to the mix of ancient Egyptian knowledge and Greek philosophical wisdom that emerged from 500 BC through to 01 AD. They were probably the basis of the emerging religious dynasty and somehow survived the efforts to exterminate everything that preceded them. The texts are extraordinarily prophetic with very accurate descriptions of the 96 per cent and offer incredible spiritual insights. These insights are called gnosis, which means mysterious divine knowledge.

In the Key, there is a lovely description of how soul, spirit and mind are arranged within us. The human being is made up of layers that withdraw into the centre upon death, one at a time, from the outside in. Imagine four circles of decreasing size all sitting inside one another. The outer circle is the body. The next circle in is the spirit. The circle within this is the limit of the soul and this surrounds the smallest circle that represents the mind. In this way, the mind is in the soul, which is in the spirit, which is in the body. At death the spirit pulls inward from the outer body, pulling out of its veins and heart and withdrawing into the soul and then the mind only. "And then the mind, stripped of wrappings and naturally divine takes unto itself a fiery body" and ascends. From there it assumes an energy state that is too refined or rare for us to comprehend. However, when mind, spirit and soul are together within us, mind will pull together with soul and spirit, becoming the motivation and energy of God that we can express and work with.

The Key gives a hierarchy of deity, with a single creator or God at the top, multiple gods and goddesses underneath and nature below them. Then comes human beings who control "arts and science".

The trouble is we took control of "arts and science" and then took them too far. We introduced more and more gadgets, systems and complexity, which requires a great amount of planetary resources. But worse, we stopped believing in the gods and goddesses. We thought we could just report straight to the top man and the consequential monotheism led us into very misguided spiritual beliefs. We even have evidence of this in the Bible, which I pointed out in chapter four. When this top God planted the Garden of Eden, why did he have something there that could, and did, spoil his idyll? He must have *had* to accept it. This tree represents the deities.

Unfortunately, the leaders of the world's biggest religions took the single god at the top and ran with that at the expense of the multiple gods and goddesses in the middle rankings. It doesn't work like that. You can't miss them out. You have to work with them or they will make themselves known, as they are doing now. There is no quick way to the top, missing out the middle management. *For they are the 96 per cent.* And although, as I said, they will protect humanity for its enviable, independent self-governance, they will ultimately demand their share of the action too. If not, they will disrupt everything and then it will all have to start again.

We need to love our planets and their deities and then they will love us back!

11

THE CRAZY PHENOMENON OF 2012

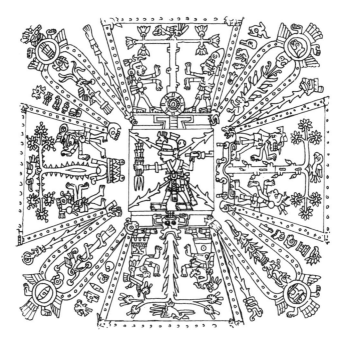

20 *The Fejervary screenfold title page*

What's really going to happen in 2012? And why are we asking ourselves that question?

We are told the world will end in a cataclysmic event foretold by a civilisation called the Maya, who lived in Middle America up to 1,000 years ago. According to students of the Maya, a certain calendar of theirs runs out on 21st December 2012, so this is when it will happen. Well, *my* calendar runs out a few days later than that every year, but it doesn't make me think that the world will end. I just start a new calendar and I think it is worth dwelling on that point.

It should also be noted that the prophecy of a doomsday event and the ending of the calendar are two separate issues and there is nothing to imply that one is connected to the other. They have just been put together by Mayan fans with no real basis for this correlation. That in itself is enough to cast real doubt on the whole thing, but close inspection of other claims regarding events in the cosmos are also doubtful.

This chapter has been written as an addendum to the original edition because of the fear that erupted in 2009 and in it we examine all the pertinent information and then look at the astrology of the situation for some answers. My overall impression is that there is no cataclysmic event, or any need to fear 21st December 2012.

The Maya

The Mayan dynasty existed in the area of Middle or Mesoamerica that is now Guatamala and Mexico. They rose to power around 300 AD before declining in strength around 900 AD (possibly due to over-consuming natural resources) and so had a similar timeline to the Romans in Europe. There is evidence of human settlement in the Americas going as far back as 10,000 BCE[1] and in Mexico in particular from around 9,000 BCE. But the more recent evidence was from a civilisation called the Olmecs who occupied Mesoamerica around 1,500 BCE and the Maya absorbed some of their knowledge.

For despite the fact they existed for roughly only 600 years, the Maya had an extraordinary ability to accurately calculate and record immense passages of time covering millions of years and they developed many sophisticated and ingenious calendars and counts to assist them with this. According to one author[2], they had 21 or more different cycles, counts or calendars running at the same time. Some were based on a very precise knowledge of the movement of the planets and others were the addition of days parcelled up into longer periods of time, like our years, centuries and millennia. They had Tuns, Katuns, Baktuns and Piktuns which comprised of 360 days, 7,200 days, 144,000 days and 2,880,000 days respectively. There were even bigger counts, some concerning events that happened millions of years ago, but we aren't really concerned with those since it is the Baktun count of 144,000 days that some Mayanists think may end and start anew in December 2012. They say we are currently in the 12th Baktun, which began in 1618 and ends around 21st December 2012 when the 13th Baktun begins.[3] Although even this is under scholarly debate.

It is important to note that all the other counts restart at the same time. There are two broad groups within which counts are constantly ending and beginning in their own rhythm irrespective of each other. One is synchronised with the planets, the other with the addition of days.

The Maya also had a World Age Creation myth that describes how the world has been repeatedly created and destroyed by flood, fire and terrible demons and it is this destructive aspect that the doomsday seekers of today have latched on to and tried to connect to the end of the Baktun count. However, there is no basis for this correlation and no evidence that the end of this cycle is one of these world age creation points talked about in the World Age Creation myth. That in itself should be enough to enough to allay any fears about the end of the world in 2012.

One academic[4] states that the end of a Baktun was always simply about great change as the Maya demonstrated at the end of the last one in 1618. Another author[5] states that there is also no record of how the Maya actually celebrated the end of any of their counts, but he describes what the Aztecs did, who were their later neighbours. His account is about the end of an Aztec 52 year cycle. Apparently, they would prepare for a symbolic 'end of the world' by extinguishing all fires, sweeping their homes and throwing statues into water. They would then celebrate the new beginning by massing at the nearest high point so the priests/astrologers could climb up to get a view of the stars and crucially the horizon for prediction of the future. Fire was kindled and freshly lit torches of it were distributed to re-light all the fires of the temple and homes. This is more a new beginning than an ending and certainly astrology always views things in this way. We don't call the end of the Moon's cycle around our planet an 'Old' Moon, we call it a 'New' Moon. Similarly, we have a New Year not an Old Year.

Only four Mayan documents survived the Christian purging by the Spanish, and each is astrological in nature. Astrological understanding requires an appreciation of cycles but these are not meant to be interpreted as endings as in 'end-of-time', they are instead symbolic of new beginnings. Lots of the Mayan cycles were taken from the movement of the planets which can be seen from Earth. However, the particular cycle which is causing all the fuss was not part of that group. The Baktun Long Count is simply a multiple of days, as in revolutions of the Earth. So adding them up and calling them spiritually important is like adding up the days in a millennium and calling that spiritually important. A great time for a party and yes, we did all know it was coming, but did we get hysterical about it before hand? Now I think about it, yes we did. Remember the millennium bug and computer clocks?

It is also important to understand that prediction is made within the framework and context of the times it is made in. It can only be expressed in that terminology. Centuries later we assume different outcomes because we start from a different environment with different spiritual awareness. What may at one time be described as burning hell fires, we may now predict as profoundly positive spiritual evolution. The same planetary configuration describes both.

What does the Mayan prophecy actually say?

As stated previously there is no evidence of any doomsday endings specifically reported for the end of the Baktun cycle in December 2012. In fact there is only one specific prophecy relating to this date and that is harmless. According to one author,[6] the inscription was found at a place called Tortuguero in Mexico. It mentions the end point of the 13th Baktun cycle, but the left wing of the stone cross is missing and the central section is damaged. He says the prophecy also has a big crack in it so "full translation is virtually impossible" but they think it is:

" ...will occur. The descent of the nine support gods to the... "

That is it I'm afraid. That is the only real prediction regarding what will happen at the end of the 13th Baktun count. And note it says end of the Baktun count. Some scholars say 2012 marks the beginning of the 13th Baktun count. Very confusing.

According to one source,[7] there is an inscription that refers to the last culmination of the 13th Baktun cycle on 13th August 3114 BCE and it is not about destruction, it is about creation. There is an ordering of the gods, the forming of a central hearth and a planting of stones. This stone tablet also informs of mythic stuff well before 3114 BCE so it obviously informs about a continuing cycle.

A look at the various claims made about 2012

Astronomers making predictions! Whatever next?

Some astronomers have put forward a few predictions of their own. Mike Brown[8] has declared "the world is not going to end in 2012" and even NASA has joined in with a confident "2012… won't be the end of the world" and "nothing bad will happen to the Earth in 2012".[9] Of course, it is possible to point out with some irony that these statements are also predictions!

Does the Chinese I Ching agree the modern Mayan doomsday theory?

There is another claim that a Chinese tool of prophecy, called the I Ching also flags up this date, so giving weight to the Mayan prediction, but there is no certainty about which date in our calendar corresponds to a date in theirs. A TV programme called '2012, on the Edge' featured Geoff Stray explaining how they had matched the prediction of a big, one-off event in the I Ching calendar to one here on Earth. The thinking was that if they got one day that corresponded to both, then that would match them up completely. The earthly event they chose was the dropping of an atom bomb on Japan. Having aligned the calendars in this way, they then point out that the Chinese end date falls on 21st December 2012. Pick another earthly event to match the calendars up with and of course, the Chinese end date falls on a different day, so this theory is wide open to criticism.

Galactic Alignment stuff

OK, what on earth is a Galactic Alignment? Well, this one supposedly describes how the equator of our Galaxy is in an imaginary line with the Sun and the Earth on the winter solstice of the northern hemisphere which is on 21st December 2012.

However, this is not the sensation claimed. To start with, there is real doubt as to where the exact equator of the Galaxy is since we don't really know precisely where the edges are.[10] No-one has been outside the Solar System, let alone the Galaxy, to take a look. We also have to remember that the Galaxy is a collection of hundreds of billions of stars, so how can it have a line round it? However the IAU has approved a co-ordinates system, re-drawn in the 1960s, which gives the Galaxy lines, like latitude and longitude lines here on Earth. One of these lines, the central one, is called the Galactic Equator, but it is just a line for mapping purposes, and has no importance in astrology.

Furthermore, if this 'alignment' between the Earth, Sun and Galactic Equator is important at all, then we should understand that whatever it represents has already happened.[11] The line-up that shows the significance of 21/12/2012 has been happening twice a year for decades. In fact it was most exact in 1998, but it occurs twice a year from 1980 until 2016. It happens twice a year because there is a solstice on 21st June and 21st December.

The line the IAU calls the Galactic Equator pierces the *centre* of the Galaxy at one point, but that fact does not make the whole line spiritually important. It's just a line used to mark out the sky so that astronomers can measure it. Let's look at an illustration to try to understand this. Say that London is spiritually and physically important as the centre of somewhere. The imaginary Greenwich meridian line, which is another line in a co-ordinates system just like the Galactic Equator line, runs straight through it. The line, which is labelled 0° longitude, runs from the South Pole to the North Pole and goes through London at Greenwich. Now, if you walk across that imaginary line somewhere in Scotland, it does not make your crossing spiritually important does it? This is the claim that some Mayan fans are making.

There are other claims that the *centre* of the Galaxy (which is not the same thing as the equator) is lined up with the Sun and Earth during the December 2012 solstice. Now, the centre of the Galaxy is *very* important. It is a spot in the middle of our Galaxy, which emits unusual radio signals and very likely has a black hole which regulates[12] our whole Galaxy of hundreds of billions of stars or suns. In astrology we have long known that the centre of the Galaxy amplifies the power of anything that is in its direction. However the claim that the centre of the Galaxy, the Sun and the Earth are in alignment on the 21st December 2012 is wrong.[13] They are roughly four degrees apart, and this is too big a gap to make the 21st Dec important. The centre of the Galaxy is at about 26° of Sagittarius and the Sun will be at 0° Capricorn. Therefore they are *not* in line at the solstice. These days, the Sun is in line with the Galactic centre about four days *before* the solstice actually, but generally there is always an alignment twice a year at some point during the Earth's orbit around the Sun. This has happened since the formation of the Solar System and is completely normal. The solstice point of 0° Capricorn will eventually 'precess' or 'wobble' back to the

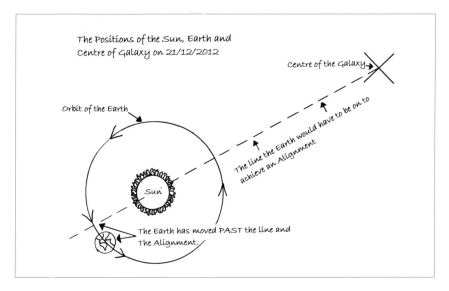

The Positions of the Sun, Earth and Centre of Galaxy on 21/12/2012

Centre of the Galaxy

Orbit of the Earth

The Line the Earth would have to be on to achieve an Alignment

Sun

The Earth has moved PAST the line and The Alignment.

21 *This simple diagram can't give an impression of height, but if it could we would see that the dotted line goes under the under the Galaxy Centre and so there isn't a really exact joining of the centres this way either. But in astrology, we accept this as being exact and those rules have stood for centuries*

centre of the Galaxy, meaning, there will come a day when the Earth is on that line on the 21st December, but not for another 200 years or so.[14]

So the 'Galactic Alignment' theory is not valid. The facts have been stretched and manipulated until they are just not correct any more. The galactic alignment they talk of does not happen for another 200 years or so. The astronomy has been over-enthusiastically misconstrued. Perhaps it might have been more prudent to use terms like "in the vicinity of" and not "alignment".

I take nothing away from the importance and severity of the issues that the human race does face in the 21st century. Climate change, dwindling bio-diversity, potential world financial collapse, food security, rampant consumerism etc. and these are without doubt very worrying times, but at least our awareness means we can make attempts to rectify them. So, in recognising that we do have worrying issues and these are indeed challenging times, did the Maya have knowledge enough to try to warn us? Considering all the planet-threatening events that have occurred so far, why not leave warning about them too? Did they leave us detailed warning about Krakatoa erupting in 1883, or the comet strike at Tunguska in 1908? Or how about the mini ice age in Europe, the two World Wars, the 2004 tsunami?

Planet Nibiru will hit earth

There is a theory that a non-existent or unknown planet called Nibiru will hit Earth and it is tempting to see this as a really good science fiction idea. But in truth there was an incident in July 2009 when a very large comet must have hit Jupiter and none of the world's space agencies even noticed until the hole appeared in the side of the planet. However, I don't think they would miss a whole planet.

The Sumerians originally wrote of the mythical planet Nibiru. They lived in the region of Iraq between 7,000 and 4,000 BCE and are considered to be the first highly advanced master race. Fortunately, tablets inscribed with their creation myth have survived to this day and we are lucky enough to have good translations. The hero, Marduk, symbol of the light, future, mankind, and masculine energy, battles Tiamat, a fierce Mother Nature, darkness, or feminine energy. (For more on Tiamat, see chapter four.) The simple everyday occurrence of the Earth rolling out of the dark night and towards the light may have stimulated this symbolism, which has a more modern day equivalent in the myth of Hercules and the Hydra, or the story of George and the Dragon.

Nibiru is mentioned only *once*. The indexes of several academic books on the Sumerians, including the rare and comprehensive '*Ancient Near East Texts*' by Pritchard, reveal just the one reference which occurs in the Creation myth. here are three different translations:

"Merodach set all the great gods in their several stations. He also created their images, the stars of the Zodiac, and fixed them all. He measured the year and divided it into months; for twelve months he made three stars each. After he had given starry images of the gods separate control of each day of the year, he founded the station of Nibiru (Jupiter), his own star, to determine the limits of all stars, so that none might err or go astray. He placed beside his own the stations of Enlil and Ea, and on each side he opened mighty..."[15]

"...the star, which shineth in the heavens.
May he hold the Beginning and the Future, may they pay homage unto him, saying, "He who forced his way through the midst of Tiamat without resting,
Let his name be Nibiru, 'the Seizer of the Midst'!
For the stars of heaven he upheld the paths,
He shepherded all the gods like sheep!
He conquered Tiamat, he troubled and ended her life."[16]

"Nebiru shall hold the crossings of heaven and earth; those who failed of crossing above and below, ever of him shall inquire. Nebiru is the star which in the skies is brilliant. Verily he governs their turnings, to him indeed they look, saying "He who the midst of the sea restlessly crosses, let 'Crossing' be his name, who controls its midst. May they uphold the course of the stars of heaven; May he shepherd all the gods like sheep. May he vanquish Tiamat, may her life be strait and short!"[17]

I challenge anyone to find the bit where it says "scary planet which will hit Earth and annihilate it in 2012."

It's interesting to read those texts and then consider what we now know of the Sun's influence over the Solar System. However, historians don't believe the Sumerians could have had such sophisticated knowledge of the Sun's gravitational pull over the rest of the planets because we think 'ancient' means primitive. They believe that the further back in time you go, the less well-informed the people were, but I am of the opinion that we devolved or lost knowledge. I believe that the Sumerians who carved the tablets of creation knew enough about the Sun to state that it was a star. "Nibiru is the star which in the skies is brilliant". And that the Sun "determine[d] the limits of all stars, so that none might err or go astray", meaning that the Sun's gravity kept all the planets in place.

Another quote for consideration is "May he vanquish Tiamat, may her life be strait and short". Our Sun vanquishes darkness (Tiamat). In other words, our Sun fuels an invisible, protective 'heliosphere' or bubble around the Solar System which holds back life-destroying gamma rays and other space chaos and could be called Tiamat. There are many ways of looking at it and the early 20th century translators assumed Nibiru to be Jupiter because of that planet's giant gravitational pull, which, along with the Sun, does indeed keep the other planets in line.

On the other hand, Venus is the most brilliant star-like object in the sky and Nibiru could be the name given to her most brilliant emanation.

The magnetic North Pole will flip, reversing polarity with the South Pole

Yes, it's possible. This happens to the Sun quite regularly and it has happened on Earth before. To understand the implications of this, we have to understand what the magnetic north pole is, and what it isn't. The Earth spins on an axis. Think of a model globe and how you can whirl it around because it spins on a metal rod. The axis of the Earth is like that metal rod and there is a point at either end of our planet which marks each end of the axis of rotation. This is the end of the 'pole'. So we have a North Pole and a South Pole and they are the 'real' ones and they can't move. Then, just to complicate matters, there

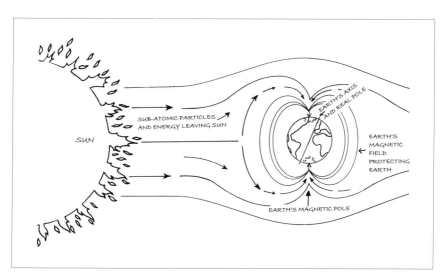

22 *Earth's magnetic poles*

is another 'pole' which arises because the Earth is like a giant magnet, with a north and south end. Do you remember those science lessons at school, when you sprinkled iron filings over a sheet of paper with a magnet underneath it? The iron filings fell in a pattern that looked like butterfly wings and this was due to the magnetic field lines around the magnet. And just as all magnets have a north and south end, so too does the Earth. But the magnetic north and south poles are not static and they move around.

A report in *National Geographic*[18] in 2006 stated that the magnetic north pole "is hightailing it towards Siberia at a clip of 25 miles a year". Since its discovery in 1831 it has moved some 700 miles and it is projected to move from Canada to Siberia in Russia within 40 years. One of the manifestations of the magnetic pole is the Aurora Borealis, the beautiful lights that appear in the far northern skies. These are due to the arrival of energetic solar wind (stuff!) from the Sun.[19] It forces sub-atomic particles to be funnelled down the magnetic poles towards the Earth. Their energy connects with other 'stuff' in the atmosphere and hey presto! Curtains of ethereal light in a ring around the magnetic north pole. These particles don't get to the rest of our planet because they are channelled away by the Earth's magnetic field which protects our planet from the worst of the solar wind.

So how important is this movement of the magnetic pole? Well, if it just wanders about, the official line is that it's probably okay, since we really don't rely on compasses any more, which have always pointed to magnetic north. Our Global Positioning System (GPS) uses satellites.

But there is something more that we should take into account. If the magnetic poles of the Earth wander around so much that they actually 'flip', it means that north becomes south and south becomes north. This is known as magnetic field reversal[20] and according to the Georgia State University website, there is evidence that it has happened 171 times in 71 million years. If it should happen again, it may not be noticed by us personally because these magnetic lines aren't noticeable in human bodies, but the satellites we have in space will need protecting.

An article in *New Scientist*[21] in 1996 stated that the last flip was 780,000 years ago and suggested we were therefore due another one since they have happened about every 500,000 years. It also reported evidence of one flip that happened at the rate of six degrees per day. Since it has to move 180 degrees in total, it would therefore theoretically take about a month to happen, but this is vehemently denied by some scientists who talk in terms of years. However long it took, the protective magnetic field lines, or magnetosphere, would be weakened and in disarray, leaving the Earth vulnerable to receiving the damaging solar wind. The resulting magnetic storms, which usually cause the Aurora, would then happen all over the planet and not just at the poles. This would affect our satellites and therefore all communications. Our vulnerability in this respect is well known and hopefully safeguards are being put in place.

Since all migratory species use the magnetic field lines to find their way around this may cause them some initial difficulty. However it seems they are better equipped for this than we are, because they have an apparent 'software update' mechanism hard-wired into their brains. According to another *New Scientist*[22] report published in 2008, birds re-align their magnetic line-reading capabilities when that special blue light of dusk and dawn appears. That makes *so* much sense of the spiritual importance of dawn and dusk and also explains the dawn chorus. It has also been found that tuna fish the world over always dive to the ocean floor when the Sun is in that position compared to where they are, meaning they perform these 'spike' dives when the Sun is six degrees (about half an hour in time) below the horizon. Apparently, "At this time of their day, magnetic interference created by solar wind is at its lowest", so they will be able to 'tune' into the Earth's magnetic field lines under the best conditions. This amazing capability to 'update' their software seems to be in their DNA. This was tested further in October 2009,[23] when *New Scientist* wrote that experiments carried out on robins reported that a flock easily coped with a magnetic north flip of 120° and did so using their eyes to 'see' the magnetic field lines. Such magical creatures! All this is Mother Nature's way of ensuring that life on Earth can cope with changes in the magnetic field.

The Sun should be very active with sunspots

The last doomsday prophecy worth looking at is the one about the Sun, because it sounds credible and has some science behind it.

Our Sun seems to go through an 11 year cycle of greater or lesser sunspot activity. The periods of higher activity are important because they produce much more electromagnetic 'stuff' which hits the Earth and affects our weather, and communication. This cycle is proving to be unreliable though, because the Sun should have been half way between low and high periods in 2009, but was still in a low period. Back in 2007, it was estimated that the Sun should reach a high activity period in 2010 or 2011, then that was revised to 2012 when things didn't seem to be going according to plan. Nobody really knows when it will happen. As long as the satellites are given protection, there shouldn't be too much of a problem, since this cycle repeats every 11 years and we are still here.

Actual astrological events for 2012

Astrology shows that there were always going to be challenges and fears in the years between 2008 and 2012. These could be real, as in climate change, over-population and a fragile world financial situation, or imaginary as in the Mayan doomsday prophecies.

Maybe the disinformation about 2012 was useful because it made a percentage of the population nervous enough to start caring about life on our planet. We have become technologically self-gratifying and disconnected from nature and her cycles. Maybe the reported end of a Mayan cycle awakened people to a greater appreciation of them. Life on Earth is embedded in cycles which means it must experience the 'down' side at some point. The winter or dying back part of the cycle has to happen too. If the industrialised nations were heading in a direction that was not sustainable to Mother Nature, then they would come up against her natural cycle, and they would not win, for a correction has to happen. Great civilisations have come and gone and none has survived her relentless cycles, although Mankind itself *has*.

The Divine works in mysterious ways, and a way to focus much attention on 2012 was found, even if the initial facts were wrong. Had we not had a huge amount of publicity from the media devoted to 2012 we may not have thought about our polluting, resource-wasting, spiritually-denying tracks. So, if the spiritual population was scared of a doomsday, and the scientific population was scared of climate change, and the financiers were scared of losing their money... this means we have a population ready for change and enlightenment. But what sort of enlightenment? To find the answer, we must look to the spiritual signposts which are embedded in that which is closest to us, the environment, the Sun, Moon, stars and planets.

Venus passes across the face of the Sun

On 6th June 2012, the planet Venus will pass across the face of the Sun. This is among the rarest of planetary alignments and only seven such events[24] have occurred since the invention of the telescope, in 1631, 1639, 1761, 1769, 1874, 1882, and 2004. These years are in pairs, for the event happens twice in eight years and then not again for over 100 years. It just so happens that we are living in a time when a pair of crossings will happen. There was one in 2004 and the second of the pair will happen in June 2012.[25] It should be pointed out that Venus's meetings (conjunctions) with the Sun are a common occurrence, but normally she would pass by the Sun either higher or lower. It is Venus crossing the face of the Sun that makes the 2012 event so important.

Venus is the brightest object in the sky after the Sun and Moon[26] and was of equal importance to many ancient races. She is much nearer the Sun than we are and so from the Earth it seems as if she is always either side of it; travelling before the Sun when she is the Morning Star or after it when she is the Evening Star. When she is very close to the Sun she is in the same Zodiac sign and in harmony with the Sun's energy. When she is as far away as she can get, she is in a different Zodiac sign and there is disharmony. The Sun is pouring forth one element and she subscribes to another. Human beings who are born at such times have difficulty trying to satisfy both compulsions. Ancient civilisations were also aware that her influence changed according to whether she was the Morning or Evening Star, never mind which Zodiac sign she was in.

Venus was revered because of what she represented in astrology. She was known as a vital reproductive force and she stimulated virility and success, even in war. Her influence celebrates earthly pleasure, but also the accumulation of wealth and objects of desire. For this reason it was vital to be able to predict where Venus would be in relation to the constellations and her position as the Morning or Evening Star. If she rose before the Sun in the morning she was more aggressive and warlike, symbolising power, leadership and malevolence. As the Evening Star she could be a symbol of fertility, death, old age and benevolence to the human race.[27] The theme of duality comes up again since she was so utterly dual in nature, some races even knew her as two separate deities.

We can't really say that the ending of the Mayan Baktun count pointed to Venus's passage across the face of the Sun in 2012, because the Maya fans insist it is only that single day on 21st December that is important and Venus does this in June. But it's an amazing coincidence because Venus was incredibly important to the Mayans. Success or failure in battle or with crops could depend on her support. Her passage across the face of the Sun can be seen with the naked eye at dawn or dusk and would have been very significant to the ancients who saw such events in the sky as indicating important events here on Earth. So what important events could happen? To find this out, we can look at the events that happened around the previous pairs of Venus transits.

Events around the last three pairs of Venus transits

From 1631 to 1639 Europe was being torn apart by the 30 year war in which nations were plundered and ruined.[28] Villages were ransacked and the European population was halved, but despite that, a new world view was beginning. Galileo wrote a book stating that the Earth was not the centre of the Universe, the Sun was. He was summoned to Rome by the Inquisition and taken into custody. One of the emerging influences was Rene Descartes who "brought order to thought... this was a revolution in the intellectual life of Western man".[29]

The Catholic Church remained powerful, but now it could be challenged. A new generation of scientists were disproving theories that had been accepted for generations. They sought answers to motion and dynamics; things that had been unquestioned because they were holy and under God's control. Now science demanded human investigation and, therefore, control. Authority, power and establishment were shattered or shifted. Prosperous merchant classes challenged the power of the old aristocracy and feudalism... and chocolate had arrived!

From 1761 to 1769 After a year of military successes in 1759, Britain signed peace treaties with France and Spain in 1763. Britain was now the dominant power in North America. However, the American Revolution started at this time and the Anglican Church was ousted in 1761. Exploration began with Captain Cook's mission to Tahiti and he made an unprecedented contribution to knowledge of the Pacific. An industrial revolution occurred in Britain and the first of the factories were opened. Catherine the Great ruled Russia, and Japan also had a female monarch.

From 1874 to 1882 The American Civil War had ended nine years previously so there was no association at all. According to the BBC history timeline, the most war-like events occurring worldwide involved thousands of Bulgarians being slain by the Turks and North American Indians were fighting for their lives against the white settlers. The British were exploring Africa and in 1878 they invaded Afghanistan. The Theosophical Society and the Christian Science movement were both founded in 1875.

There were huge advances in many areas of technology, such as the invention of the telephone, light bulb, and recording equipment.

Do those three periods give us events which contain useful information?

Considering Venus's ancient associations with war-like behaviour I had been expecting some kind of correlation with periods of major world war, but this was not the case.

A common feature, however, is the seeking of scientific knowledge and exploration. As this is written in 2009, it is very apparent that we are in the middle of huge advancements in scientific exploration and so this concurs with the history around these Venus transits. It is interesting to note the gathering of species and detailed illustration that was done on Captain Cook's expeditions. This painstaking recording of information marked a change in the acquisition of knowledge unknown since the demise of the classical Greek era. Astrologically, this is attributable to the two Zodiac signs in which the Venus transits occur. Gemini and Sagittarius are all about exploration and the gathering of knowledge in an effort to gain gnosis and superiority. Religion and spiritual questioning is associated with the sign of Sagittarius and each of the eras has notable milestones concerning issues of faith.

The last common theme is revolution. In the 17th century it was about scientific revolution which the Catholic Church could no longer contain. In the 18th century it was about an industrial revolution in Britain, then the dominant world super-power, and a government revolution in America. In the 19th century a technological or electrical revolution began.

Bring on the revolution!

A better way of describing it would be that we need to revolutionise many areas of the way we conduct ourselves on this planet. As this is written in the winter of 2009, the world faces enormous problems. We are heavily over-populated with resulting challenges for food production and fresh water. Industrial growth, which funds western lifestyles and social care, was funded by credit which threatens to bankrupt the western world, and the scientists at the Large Hadron Collider are going to create a black hole in Switzerland. But wait, that could be it. We need another scientific and industrial revolution. For nothing else at this stage could change the direction of mankind more comprehensively. It's what we need, and indeed, the planets describe it. We urgently need it to find a way of producing limitless, free, nonpolluting energy. These Venus transits have previously coincided with periods of exploration and the gathering of knowledge and we could do with another one of those to get us out of this mess. The particle science being explored by the teams at the Large Hadron Collider could take us into the realms of harnessing the strong nuclear force found in an atom or even energy from the 96 per cent and this could solve many problems. The right plans have now been put in place in America. During the Bush administration scientific research was under-funded, but the election of Obama has changed that. Perhaps discovery in green technologies and nuclear power can really help us now.

The other revolution experienced during those three Venus transits was spiritual and again, it may be time for such a change. In the first chapter we are told that from 2004, people who listen to angels and go to reiki classes were aware of "changes to earth consciousness" or "ascendance to higher dimensions". Well now we know why. Because changes in one sphere of human consciousness will always be synchronous with rapid growth in another. It's all connected in the great web. If we listen to our gods and goddesses we may be guided into a revolution that enables us to live in harmony with our planet. But first, perhaps we will have to cease to pray at the altar of greedy financial growth without regard to Mother Nature.

So, vive la revolution!

Wrong solstice?

The Maya fans insist that the end date is 21st December 2012, but I'm not so sure that is the date we will continue to keep our eyes on. The astrology is very much more concentrated on the first solstice of that year, which is on 21st June 2012 and there is a plausible explanation as to why the solstice of June could rightfully be called the Winter Solstice too! The seasons in the two hemispheres are opposite, so when it is winter in England it is summer in Australia. The two solstice dates are the same in each hemisphere, i.e. around the 21st June and 21st December, but the date takes its name from the accompanying season. So, the summer solstice is during the June date in the Northern Hemisphere, but during the December date in the Southern Hemisphere. And transversely, the winter solstice is in December in North America, but in June in lower parts of South America.

So what if the information for these Counts of the Maya came from an earlier civilisation, one that lived below the Equator, in Peru, 8,000 years before the Olmecs and Maya? And what if the symbol for Winter Solstice was carried over the equator into Middle America where it would be misinterpreted to mean the December solstice, not the June one? There is no evidence, except that the astrology for the June one is so much stronger.

Astrological symbolism started in 2008

Astrology seems to point to a slow evolution of events and changes that lead up to and through 2012, then on through the next four years until at least 2016. All the events that happen between 2008 and 2016, including 2012, are part of the transformation and there is no single catastrophic event, more a series of steps with a goal in mind. The celestial dance moves seamlessly from one highlight to another as if all in the same musical with different actors becoming more or less important at different times. But for this whole period there are planetary links, so that even though a large time frame is involved, it can be seen as the same dance within the musical; with different partners coming and going, rather than a new scene beginning. There is no doubt that it is a difficult and challenging time for the human race. There will have to be a lot of deconstruction and changes in attitude before reconstruction and new growth can begin.

There are peaks of action, such as the summer of 2010, but the tension produces something important. Something enlightening and generative is being forced out within the Collective. For the years leading up to this period had been about rapid industrial growth and expansion built on credit, over-consumption, pollution, waste and disconnection from planetary cycles. Earthy realism must follow such recklessness and this will force individuals and governments to be more careful with the Earth's resources. The predominating signature is one of intense dynamic movement as collective and personal attitudes have to go through considerable change. The energies concerned push each other on into revolutionary higher and noble concepts. Perhaps resource and energy-saving scientific breakthroughs. Perhaps established world order and even the 'free market' conditions will have to change. One of the planets involved in this testing is Pluto, and as we saw in chapter four, he is quite capable of razing stuff to the ground with his purification process. So anything mired in old fashioned practices may well come apart. If so, it is only to allow healthier growth, but probably in a different direction. By 2010 Pluto had already challenged the world's financial edifices and people were shocked at how easily giant global companies and banks[30] collapsed. But at least Western governments are trying to change a system that is 'too big to fail' and yet threatens the financial security of ordinary people. There is an atmosphere primed for such ground-breaking change and newness. Entrenched views will be challenged, but on the other hand the genius of the Collective can be revealed. Inspiration, awakening, power and light can flow freely in the ether, bringing new concepts in technology and government. There is potential for a symbolic birth of all that is innovative and revolutionary. Nuclear science and technology will be breaking news but the whole thing has a Berlin wall feel to it and the blueprint for a Brave New World emerges. There is an honesty about these energies, so fundamental cornerstones of how-we-did-it-before will be questioned and rightfully so. The rut of squandering and lethargy must give way to original, futuristic and revolutionary concepts for the brotherhood of Mankind. These are potentially very exciting times!

Concerning the year of 2012 itself, there is more emphasis on change in the summer than the winter and in fact by December 21st Pluto will have linked up harmoniously with Saturn. They will each empower the other to bring forth magic and the re-building will be in full swing. From November 2012 and for most of 2013, the planets that signified world financial crisis and melt down are drawing from deep reserves of constructive and life enhancing energies that facilitate and coax each other into rich rewards. There is emergence in the structure of civilisation and they build on a fundamental mastery of the deeply profound. Something presently unknown or from deep within the Collective unconscious emerges. The reality behind the perceived reality is exposed. Perhaps the breakthrough we so desperately need regarding an unlimited pollution-free energy source finally happens. There isn't a single problem in our lives today that can't be improved by harnessing the strong nuclear force in an atom. If we were able to draw power from thin air we could solve many of the problems in the world. Given sufficient eco-friendly power, we could provide all the fresh water we need by desalinating sea water and wouldn't that solve some food security challenges!

Some final thoughts about the necessity to experience collective fear concerning 2012

The Collective has leapt upon the doomsday predictions and their connections to a date in 2012 because it needs a tangible expression of the challenge that really exists in the world. These things affect the psyche of the human race and an archetypal fear of extinction raises its head. The population succumbs to an irrational fear rather than the known rational ones. After all, those involving ancient mystic prediction are the scariest of all. However, in view of the list of very real threats to the human race, an end and a beginning would be perfect! How about an end to all that pollution and over-commercialism and a beginning to a new way of living and using the Earth?

Outrageous and frightening fantasies are simply metaphors from the Collective unconscious. It is commonly accepted in psychology that dreams of cataclysm and apocalypse often precede times of great revelation, evolution and sea change in the personal consciousness of a human being. Perhaps the psyche cannot accurately translate the perceived 'thunderstorm' on the horizon, so it just imagines the worst and works back from that. According to Carl Jung, the Collective works in a similar way with certain members of society mouth-piecing the fear. The Collective gets worked up just like a human being does.

So does the idea of change on a big scale frighten you? Consider the following facts. We have to produce more food in the next 50 years than we did during the last 10,000. We have nearly exhausted the planet's raw materials. Western countries are technically bankrupt and extinction of species is happening at an accelerated rate.

We need to change drastically, and thank goodness the planets confirm sufficient quantities of change to make a difference.

Stand back… The Indigos come into their own!

In the late 1980s and early 1990s a generation was born who have already defined themselves as different, some more strongly than others. They have an older, wiser or different attitude and a superior strength of mind which is dismissive of attempts to tame it into mainstream ways of thinking. They have certain traits which astrology tells us are lying latent in their generational unconscious and will be revealed strongly from early 2012 to 2016.

Firstly, they are here to change the fundamental vision and ideals of the whole human race. They have views on love, social structure, authority, values and religious beliefs that are probably far more realistic than those of the Western industrial nations in the second half of the 20th century. These views are entangled with mystical yearning so strong they will endure hardship to build the Golden Age whose blueprint appears to be hidden in their DNA, awaiting the switch on. Their self-sufficiency and preferred isolation is really a determination to remain uncontaminated and dismissive of their parental upbringing.

They have strong focus and potential for mastery, although this is small comfort for the mother who cannot believe she has just been spoken to so sneeringly and dismissively.

Thankfully this generation sees the mystical power of the numinous in solid matter and they happily accept that there is a reality behind the perceived reality. Their minds are open to the fact that matter has intelligence, that God exists in a tree and the spiritual meaning of the Universe can be found in planets around the Sun or electrons round a nucleus. Their unique view point allows them to accept that the nature of the physical universe is not what it seems; in fact they *know* it isn't. They are desperately disappointed and disillusioned and will happily adapt to a new view of the Universe... in fact they can't wait, it's exciting and it's what they came here for.

They have new values for sacredness, loving and meaningful faith. They view the current world as too cold, disposable and lacking in spiritual appreciation and meaning.[31] They are painfully aware of a split between the clear, cold logic of science and the euphoria of fusion and harmony with a loving, compassionate and unconditional divinity. They will find both, but only when they have brought these two very separate worlds together.

Know thyself!

"A great thinker, after studying all the philosophies and sciences known at that time, came to a Seer of Truth and said: "Sir, I am tired of this lower knowledge that can be gained from books or through the study of the world of phenomena; it no longer satisfies me, for science cannot reveal the ultimate Truth; I wish to know that which is the highest. Is there anything by knowing which I can know the reality of the Universe?" The sage replied: "Yes, there is; and that knowledge is the highest, by knowing which you can know the true nature of everything in the Universe." And he continued, "Know thyself. If thou

canst learn the true nature of thine own self, thou wilt know
the reality of the Universe. In thy true self thou wilt find
the Eternal Truth, the Infinite Source of all phenomena. By
knowing this thou wilt know God and His whole creation."
As by knowing the chemical properties of one drop of water,
we know the properties of all water wherever it appears, so by
knowing who and what we are in reality, we shall realise the
final truth. Man is the epitome of the universe. That which
exists in the macrocosm is to be found in the microcosm.
Therefore the knowledge of one's true self is the highest of all
knowledge."[32]

In her book "The Outer Planets and the Collective", astrologer Liz
Greene agrees with Carl Jung that the Collective, or human race, is the
sum total of all the individuals and there is an unconscious link from
all of us into some great Universal consciousness which takes two-way,
psychic traffic. This book was written in 1980 and since then we have
discovered the 96 per cent, so we can understand more fully how this
individual soul or spirit connection to the Universal or Collective lake
of soul or spirit can exist. And since it is two-way traffic we can now
understand how our own self awareness and spiritual understanding can
contribute to the strength, wisdom and well-being of the Collective soul,
as well as giving us personal peace. Greene suggests that catastrophic
events in the Collective would not need to happen if everyone were
prepared to work with their own self-awareness, as painful as this so
often is. She says: "If I am prepared to work with my own agony, and
you are prepared to work with yours, then maybe the Collective won't
have to plunge itself into blind agony."[33]

That's one good reason to go for self awareness and here's another
more selfish one. Greene says of Carl Jung: "He seems to suggest
that when something is due to erupt in the Collective, the only safety
and sanity to be found is in the firm sense of your own individuality.

Otherwise, there is no way in which the eruption can be channelled without you becoming a victim along with the Collective."

It is a fact that those who study astrology for self awareness learn to understand and process their issues in a lot less pain than those who refuse to accept they need to be self-aware. For if people do not willingly go into the metaphorical Underworld of depth analysis then the Divine will give them 'events' to take them there anyway. And these events can be breathtakingly cruel. Better to get one step ahead and give yourself up for symbolic self-learning than have the Universe decide to teach you the same lesson, since it has to knock harder than you would to get you to listen in the first place.

After studying astrology for a while, my students always say that they feel less like a cork bobbing around in the water. Self awareness stabilises.

Obviously, I believe that astrology is able to offer an unrivalled framework for self analysis and spiritual awareness. It is worth saying again that our most important spiritual signposts are embedded in that which is closest to us in the Earth, Sun and planets and the cycles and spiritual energy they symbolise. However, you can always develop your own system. You could start by listening to the birds.

Do not fear change, embrace it

Being self-aware leads to greater ego-strength and then you fear less.

Let's look at the Mayan's attitude to beginnings. Interestingly, they usually killed something to invoke a beginning. They were acutely aware of the universal principal that something must give way for something else to begin; they hastened the beginning of the rain by offering the death of a human. Okay, perhaps we don't have to go that far, but the principle is sound. For as one door closes another always opens. To have new birth, growth and transcendence we must have the death of old attitudes and worn out, rigidly dogmatic beliefs. Carl Jung believed that great movements, sea-changes or re-birth in the Collective would be preceded by images of death since these are totally linked in the individual and Collective unconscious. Greene[34] states that she encounters clients whose dreams of earthquakes, tidal waves and great catastrophe indicate a major transformation in their spiritual growth. She speculates that clairvoyants are simply tapping into the Collective unconscious and impending change. This would make complete sense of the doomsday predictions for 2012 and what is clearly going to be a period of much needed revolution and change in attitudes.

For if we are to stop chopping down the last trees, burning the last lump of coal or fishing the last fish, we must change our attitude. With massive change, upheaval and revolution, we can correct our course and then rebuild in an environment of wisdom and discovery. We need enough change to shatter our entrenched political and national hierarchies. We need a major breakthrough in scientific understanding to allow us to take limitless green power out of thin air and for this we need to understand the reality behind the perceived reality, the nature of reality, or the reality of nature.

Hopefully the new planets have come to guide us in this, for during the course of this book, we have learnt that if the industrialised nations head in a direction that is not sustainable or in harmony with Mother Nature, then they will come up against the natural cycles. Makemake will represent the indigenous populations and 'victims' of the western way of life. He will also remind us of a spiritual faith that knows magical force exists in all things; a concept that was lost when we started worshipping a single god. We lost our relationship with the environment, when we stopped following the birds.

And now we have Eris, who gleefully fuelled 'envy politics' and started a course correction by throwing her golden apple of excessive remuneration in after the world financial crisis. Politicians were singled out first, and then, aggrieved, they started on the others. Football clubs, pharmaceutical industries and investment bankers beware. Eris is on the way!

Pluto-Charon will oversee all this; they are the ferryman and gatekeeper to the New World, beyond the revolution.

We have learnt that the planets in 2012 will empower, facilitate and coax us into a sustainable future involving a fundamental mastery and rich rewards. And why should we believe them? Because our most important spiritual signposts are embedded in that which is closest to us; the cycles of the Earth, Sun, Moon and planets.

It is very difficult for us to understand just how important the sky was to all the ancient civilisations. The stars were so much brighter then and they provided a vast television to watch at night. During the course of the night, stars and constellations appeared to travel from one side of the sky to the other. Planets, which look like stars, moved around independently and the Moon also provided a nightly story. As the Earth moves in her orbit she passes through fields of debris which looks like shooting stars or distant firework rockets and comets and fireballs appear and disappear.

The ancients were aware that the nightly soap opera in the sky coincided with the events in their daily lives, the success of their food supply and the power of their rulers. The conquests of their armies and the birth of royal children could all be predicted once they had worked out which starry event was synchronous with the earthly one. This is how astrology was born.

The planets will go on into almost infinity and their celestial dance never stops. And all we have to do to work in harmony with the Divine and follow the messengers. Most importantly, we need to look after our centre of gravity, the Earth, for she is also our spiritual centre. We have lost touch with our friends the planets, the birds and the cycles and we needed to be reminded of our obligations to them. We need to be afraid that we will lose everything before we can listen, so our fear around 2012 has been useful because it has contributed to our wake up call.

Now we must listen, or one day there may be a real 2012!

Notes and References

CHAPTER 1

[1] BLITZER, C. et al (1969) *Great Ages of Man. A History of World's Cultures. Age of Kings.* International Edition, Amsterdam: Time Inc.

[2] O'CONNER, J. J. and ROBERTSON, E. F. (Sept 1996), *Mathematical Discovery of Planets,* School of Mathematics and Statistics, University of St. Andrews, http://www-history.mcs.st-andrews.ac.uk/Indexes/Astronomy.html [Accessed 27/7/2007]

[3] BLITZER, C. et al (1969) ibid.

[4] BOURNE, J. K. (2006) The Vaulting Pole. *National Geographic,* 210(6), p24.

[5] BROWN, M. (13/7/2008) *What's In a Name (Part 2).* Mike Brown's Planets:http://www.mikebrownsplanets.com/2008/07/whats-in-name-part-2.html [accessed 6/10/2008]

[6] REANNEY, D. (1991) *The Death of Forever.* London: Souvenir Press Ltd.

CHAPTER 2

[1] CATHCART, B. (2005) The Fly in the Cathedral America: Farrar, Straus and Giroux.

[2] DAVIES, P. and GRIBBIN, J. (1991) *The Matter Myth.* St. Ives, Great Britain: Viking.

[3] LIPTON, B. Dr. (2005) *The Biology of Belief.* Llandeilo SA19 6YX UK: Cygnus Books.

[4] GEFTNER, A. (2008) Something From Nothing. *New Scientist,* Vol 199 (2674), p44.

[5] SHAPIRO et al. (2004) *Revealing The Hidden Nature of Space and Time.* Washington, D.C.: The National Academies Press.

[6] SAMPLE, I. (2008) The Idea of a Lifetime. *New Scientist,* 199 (2673), pp44–45.

[7] ANON. (27/9/2008) Nothing To LHC. *New Scientist,* 199(2675), p6.

[8] ANON. *LHC The Large Hadron Collider.* Various pages. http://lhc.web.cern.ch/lhc/ [accessed 13/10/2008]

[9] XIAO-GANG, W (2006) *Introduction to Quantum Many-boson Theory.* Articles and Lecture Notes: New States of Matter etc. Xiao-Gang Wen Home Site http://dao.mit.edu/~wen/pub/intr-frmb.pdf [Accessed 1/4/2007]

[10] WALTERS, R.J. (1997) *The Language of the Cell Cell Science.* http//w.w.w.cellscience.com/chapter.htm

[11] LIPTON, B. ibid.

CHAPTER 3

[1] WATANABE, S. (Jan 07 2002) *A Texas Sized Space Rock.* NASA http://www.jpl.nasa.gov/news/features.cfm?feature=545 [06/09/2006]

[2] GEORGE, D., BLOCH, D. (2003) *Asteroid Goddesses.* Berwick, Maine. Ibis press.

[3] SHIGA, D. (19th July 2008) Has Pluto sent us a message in Ceres? *New Scientist,* 199 (2665), p10.

[4] SEYFFERT, O. (1894) *Dictionary of Classical Antiquities.* Ceres http://www.ancientlibrary.com/seyffert/pages/0129.gif [07/09/2006]

[5] NAGY, G. (5/11/2001) (Translation of) *Homeric Hymn to Demeter.* The University of Houston http://uh.edu/~cldue/texts/demeter.html [12/8/2007]

[6] BOARDMAN, J. (1979) *Athenian Red Figure Vases of the Archaic Period.* London: Thames and Hudson.

[7] L. DA. COSTA Jr. W. Bro. Helio. (16/10/1999) The Chamber of Reflection. Grand Lodge of British Columbia. http://freemasonry.bcy.ca/texts/gmd1999/pondering.html

[8] WATTERSON, B. (1999) *Gods of Ancient Egypt.* Stroud: Sutton Publishing Ltd.

[9] BRUNTON, P. (1988) *A Search in Secret Egypt.* York Beach, Maine: Samuel Weiser, Inc.

[10] FAULKNER, R. et al (1998) *The Egyptian Book of the Dead.* San Francisco: Chronicle Books LLC.

[11] SEYFFERT, O. (1984) ibid.

[12] SAMPLE, I. (31/8/2007) *Global food crisis looms as climate change and population growth strip fertile land.* The Guardian. http://www.guardian.co.uk/environment/2007/aug/31/climatechange.food [20/7/2008]

[13] BOARDMAN, J. (1980) *Athenian Black Figure Vases.* London: Thames and Hudson.

[14] NILSSON, M. (1940) *Greek Popular Religion.* Sacred Texts. http://www.sacred-texts.com/cla/gpr/gpr07.htm [12/08/2007]

[15] KERENYI, C. and JUNG, C. (1973) Essays on a Science of Mythology, trans. in GEORGE, D and BLOCH, D. (1986) *Asteroid Goddesses.* Berwick, Maine. Ibis Press.

CHAPTER 4
[1] BULFINCH, T. (1978) *Bulfinch's Mythology.* U.S.A. Avenel.

[2] ANON. (1971) *The Living Bible.* Sussex: Tynedale House Publishers.

[3] HAND, R. (1976) *Planets in Transit: life Cycles for Living.* U.S.A. Whitford Press.

[4] BLAVATSKY, H.P. (1888) *The Secret Doctrine: The Synthesis of Science, Religion and Philosophy.* Sacred Texts. http://www.sacred-texts.com/the/sd/sd1-0-co.htm#preface [Vol1pp 459 footnotes] [accessed10/8/2008]

[5] DANIELOU, A. (1991) *The Myths and Gods of India.* Vermont: Inner Traditions Int. Ltd.

[6] DANIELOU, A. ibid. p198.

[7] WATTERSON, B. (1999) *Gods of Ancient Egypt.* Stroud: Sutton Publishing Ltd. p67.

[8] WATTERSON, B. ibid. p68.

[9] WEST, J. A. (1993) *Serpent in the Sky, The High Wisdom of Ancient Egypt.* 2nd ed., Illinois: Quest Books.

[10] WATTERSON, B. ibid.

[11] VAN DEN DUNGEN, W. (2001) *On the Shabaka Stone.* Sophiatopia. http://www.maat.sofiatopia.org/shabaka.htm [accessed 14/8/2008]

[12] CATHCART, B. (2005) *The Fly in the Cathedral.* America: Farrar, Straus and Giroux

[13] GOODMAN, L. (1987) *Linda Goodman's Star Signs.* (2nd ed.) London: Pan Books Ltd.

[14] LEO, A. (1983) *Esoteric Astrology.* (2nd ed.) Vermont: Destiny Books Ltd.

[15] GREENE, L. (1976) *Saturn, A New Look at an Old Devil.* Maine, U.S.A. Samuel Weiser, Inc.

[16] WEST, J. A. ibid. p64.

[17] ALEXANDER, A. (22nd June 2006) *Nix and Hydra Join Pluto's Family The Planetary Society.* http://www.planetary.org/news/2006/0622_Nix_and_Hydra_join_Plutos_Family.html [accessed 5/11/2006]

[18] ALEXANDER, A. (3rd November 2005) *Hubble Observations Add Two New Moons to Pluto The planetary Society.* http://www.planetary.org/news/2005/1103_Hubble_Oberservations_Add_Two_New_Moons:html [accessed 5/11/2006]

[19] BLAVATSKY, H. P. (1888) *The Secret Doctrine: The Synthesis of Science, Religion and Philosophy.* Sacred Texts:(Vol. 2, pp 488) http://www.sacred-texts.com/the/sd/sd2-2-04.htm [accessed 19/9/2008]

[20] GOODMAN, L. ibid.

[21] BOOTH, E. R. Dr. (1906) *History of Osteopathy.* Meridian Institute www.meridianinstitute.com/eant/files/booth/chapter10.htm [accessed 9/11/2006]

[22] BLANEY, Dr K. (2002) *The Caduceus Versus the Staff of Asclepius.* Dr Keith T Blaney: http://drblayney.com/Asclepius.html [accessed 15/11/2006]

[23] FICINO, A. (2001) *Late Antiquity: Hermetica.* Ralph Abraham, PhD http://www.ralph-abraham.org/ficino/newbook/ch2.pdf (p19) [accessed 14/11/2006]

[24] TEGMARK, M. *Multiverse.* Massachusetts Institute of Technology http://www.space.mit.edu/home/tegmark/multiverse1.html [accessed 8/8/08]

[25] BARTLETT, D. et al, (2003) *The Elegant Universe, Welcome to the Eleventh Dimension.* NOVA: http://www.pbs.org/wgbh/nova/transcripts/3014_elegant.html [accessed 17/2/2009]

[26] NOELS, C. 14/1/1999 *The History of the LHC Project*. LHC The Large Hadron Collider: http://lhc.web.cern.ch/lhc/general/history.htm [accessed 16/9/2008]

[27] ELBARADEI, M. Dr. (27/6/2004) *Nuclear Power: A Look At The Future*. I.A.E.A.: http://www.iaea.org/NewsCenter/Statements/2004/ebsp2004n005.html [accessed on 17/9/2008]

[28] DANIELOU, A. ibid. p217.

[29] BLANEY, Dr K., (2002) *The Caduceus Versus the Staff of Asclepius*. Dr Keith T Blaney: http://drblayney.com/Asclepius.html

[30] BROOKS, M. (2008) The Power of Belief. *New Scientist*. 199 (2670) pp26–39.

CHAPTER 5
[1] ANON. (20/6/2003) *25th Anniversary of the Discovery of Pluto's Moon, Charon*. U.S. Naval Observatory: http://www.usno.navy.mil/pao/press/charon.shtml [accessed 3/9/2008]

[2] ARNETT, B. (21/4/2008) *Charon*. The Nine Planets: http://www.nineplanets.org/pluto.html#charon [accessed 3/9/2008]

[3] ANON. (August 2006) *Planet Definition Question and Answer Sheet*; International Astronomical Union: http://www.iau.org/public_press/news/release/iau0601/q_answers/ [accessed 4/9/2008 and 18/2/2009]

[4] BULFINCH, T. (1978) *Bulfinch's Mythology*. USA Avenel.

[5] CAMPION, N. (2008) *The Dawn of Astrology*. London. Continuum Books.

[6] BULFINCH, T. ibid.

[7] RADICE, B. (1973) *Who's Who in the Ancient World*. 2nd ed., Middlesex: Penguin Books.

[8] RADICE, B. ibid.

[9] COTTERELL, A. (2000) *World Mythology*. Parragon: London.

[10] ATSMA, A. *Nyx*. THEOI Greek Mythology: http://www.theoi.com/Protogenos/Nyx.html [accessed 30/9/2008]

[11] MERCER, S (1952) Texts of Miscellaneous Contents; The Pyramid Texts: http://www.sacred-texts.com/egy/pyt/pyt49.htm

[12] PRITCHARD, J. (1955) *Ancient Near Eastern Texts Relating to the Old Testament*. 2nd Ed. New Jersey: Princeton p91.

[13] REANNY, D. (1995) *The Death of Forever*. 2nd ed., London: Souvenir Press.

[14] LINDSTROM, M. et al. (13/6/2008) *Pluto*. NASA http://solarsystem.jpl.nasa.gov/planets/profile.cfm?Object=Pluto&Display=Overview

CHAPTER 6
[1] BROWN, M. (2008) What's In a Name? Part 2. Mike Brown's Planets: http://www.mikebrowns-planets.com/2008/07/whats-in-name-part-2.html [accessed 07/10/2008]

[2] FLENLEY, J. and BAHN, P. (2002) *The Enigma of Easter Island*. New York: Oxford University Press p13.

[3] HEYERDAHL, T. (1958) *Aku-Aku The Secret of Easter Island*. 2nd ed., London: Tinling and Co. p317.

[4] SMART, N. (1989) *The World's Religions*. 2nd ed., Cambridge. Cambridge University Press.

[5] RUGGLES, C. (2005) *Ancient Astronomy*. California; ABC-CLIO.

[6] FINNEY, B. (2005) Applied Ethnoastronomy: Navigating By The Stars Across The Pacific. in CHAMBERLAIN et al. (ed) *Songs From The Sky*. United Kingdom: Oscarina Books, p336.

[7] LOW, S. *Gift of the Wind, Aboard Hokule'a on Her Miraculous Journey to Rapa Nui*. Polynesian Voyaging Society. http://pvs.kcc.hawaii.edu/rapanui/samleg3.html [accessed 23/10/2008]

[8] FLENLEY and BARN ibid. p75.

[9] FLENLEY and BARN ibid. p42.

[10] ANON. *The Statues of Easter Island. Extracts From Lectures by Thor Heyerdahl*. Bradshaw Foundation: http://www.bradshawfoundation.com/thor/index.php [accessed 14/11/2008]

[11] HEYERDAHL, T. ibid.

[12] HOLMES, B. (2006) *Did Humans Devastate Easter Island on Arrival?* New Scientist: http://www.newscientist.com/arcticle.ns?id+dn8825&print=true

[13] THOMPSON, W. (1891) *Te Pito Te Henua, Or Easter Island*. Sacred Texts: http://www.sacred-texts.com/pac/ei/ei00.htm [p463]

[14] FISCHER, S. (2005) *Island At The End of The World*. London: Reaktion Books Ltd. p50.

[15] FISCHER, S. ibid. p74

[16] YOUNG, E. (31/7/2006) Easter Island: A Monumental Collapse? *New Scientist*. com: http://www.newscientist.com/article. ns?id=mg19125621.100&print=true [accessed 23/10/2008]

[17] FISCHER, S. ibid. p89.

[18] FISCHER, S. ibid. p99.

[19] FLENLEY and BARN. ibid.

[20] THOMPSON, W. ibid. p473.

[21] THOMPSON, W. ibid. p468.

[22] THOMPSON, W. ibid. p459.

[23] ENGLERT, S. (1972) *Island At The Centre of The World*. London: Robert Hale and Co. p65.

[24] CARROLL, A. (1892) *The Easter Island Inscriptions And The Translation And Interpretation Of Them*. Journal of the Polynesian Society. http://www.rongorongo.org/carroll/105.html

[25] THOMPSON, W. ibid. p535.

[26] RJABCHIKOV, S. (1998) *Several Rongorongo Records. Symbolism of Archaic Beliefs*. Anthroglobe. http://www.anthroglobe.info/docs/Sergei/Rongorongo-records.htm [accessed 24/7/2008]

[27] FISCHER, S. ibid. p76.

[28] THOMPSON, W. ibid. p471.

[29] FISCHER, S. ibid. p73.

[30] RUGGLES, C. ibid. p140.

[31] RUGGLES, C. ibid. p407.

[32] VAN TILBERG, J. (2000) *Secrets of Easter Island, Stone Giants*: NOVA Online: http://www.pbs.org/wgbh/nova/easter/civilization/giants.html

[33] THOMPSON, W. ibid. p499.

[34] HUNT, T. and LIPO, C. (2005) Mapping Prehistoric Statue Roads on Easter Island http://www.anthropology.hawaii.edu/projects/rapanui/lipo&huntper cent202005.pdf [accessed 23/11/2008]

[35] THOMPSON, W. ibid. p498.

[36] CARROLL, A. (1892) *The Easter Island Inscriptions And The Translation And Interpretation Of Them*. Journal of the Polynesian Society. http://www.rongorongo.org/carroll/105.html [accessed 24/7/2008]

[37] ENGLERT, S. (1980) *Histories, Legends and Traditions of Easter Island*. The Rongorongo of Easter Island: http://www.rongorongo.org/leyendas/034.htm [28/10/2008]

[38] ANON. *Earthquake of Peru;* USGS: http://earthquake.usgs.gov/regional/world/peru/history.php [accessed 3/12/2008]

[39] THOMPSON, W. ibid. p499.

[40] FLENLEY and BAHN. Ibid. p15.

[41] HOLMES, B. Beastly Tales. *New Scientist*. 197(2639), pp30–33.

[42] TILBURG, J. (1994) *Easter Island, Archaeology, Ecology and Culture*. U.S.A.: Smithsonian Institution Press.

[43] ORLOVE, S. et al (2000) Forecasting Andean rainfall and crop yield from the influence of El Nino on Pleiades visibility. *Nature*, 403, pp68–71. (Kindly sent to me by Bill Law, President of the Walsall Astronomy Group.)

[44] ALLEN, M. (15/5/2007) *Three Millennia of Human and Sea Turtle Interactions In Remote Oceania*. Sea Turtle Organisation: http://74.125.77.132/search?q=cache:xUky09BYpFQJ:www.seaturtle.org/PDF/Allen_2007_CoralReefs.pdf+turtles,+polynesia.+migratory+pattern,+breeding,+ar rival&hl=en&ct=clnk&cd=1&gl=uk [accessed 24/12/2008]

[45] DE SANTILLANA, G. and VON DECHEND, H. (1969) *Hamlet's Mill. An Essay Investigating the Origins of Human Knowledge and its Transmission Through Myth*. New Hampshire. Godine Publisher Inc. p164.

[46] YOUNG, E. (12/4/2008) Ocean Biodiversity: Depths of Ignorance. *New Scientist*: http://www.newscientist.com/article/mg19826511.700-ocean-biodiversity-depths-of-ignorance.html [accessed 25/12/2008]

[47] PEARSON, A. (2009) *Perfect Storm*. New Scientist. 201(2689), pp32–35.

[48] DE SANTILANA, G. and VON DECHEND, H. (1969) *Hamlet's Mill. An Essay Investigating The Origins Of Human Knowledge And It's Transmission Through Myth*. New Hampshire: David R Godine Inc.

[49] DE SANTILANA, G. and VON DECHUND, H. (1969) ibid.

[50] BILLIMORIA, N. *The Panis of the Rig Veda and Script of Mohenjo Daro and Easter Island*. Journal of the Polynesian Society. Vol 48. http://www.rongorongo.org/theories/indus/bill092.html pp93 [accessed 26/10/2008]

[51] BILLIMORIA, N. ibid. p96.

[52] FISCHER, S. ibid. p57.

[53] YOUNG, E. (31/7/2006) Easter Island: A Monumental Collapse? *New Scientist*. com: http://www.newscientist.com/article.ns?id=mg19125621.100&print=true [accessed 23/10/2008]

[54] THOMPSON, W. ibid. p490.

[55] ENGLERT, S. ibid.

CHAPTER 7
[1] COURTLAND, R. (19/9/2008) *Controversial Dwarf Planet Finally Named Haumea;* New Scientist: http://www.newscientist.com/article/dn14759-controversial-dwarf-planet-finally-named-haumea.html

[2] McKEE, M. (29/7/2005) *New World Found in Outer Solar System;* New Scientist: http://www.newscientist.com/article/dn7751-new-world-found-in-outer-solar-system.html

[3] BROWN, M. (2006) *Haumea;* California Institute of Technology, http://www.gps.caltech.edu/~mbrown/2003EL61/

[4] SCHILLING, G. (15/10/2008) Dwarf Planet's Body Parts Litter the Solar System; *New Scientist*: http://www.newscientist.com/article/dn14954

[5] BECKWORTH, M. (1940) *Hawaiian Mythology*; Sacred Texts: http://www.sacred-texts.com/pac/hm/hm21.htm [accessed 31/1/2009]

[6] LILIUOKALANI, Queen of Hawaii, (1897) *An Account of the Creation of the World According to Hawaiian Tradition*. Sacred Texts: http://www.sacred-texts.com/pac/lku/lku01.htm [accessed 3/2/2008]

[7] BECKWORTH, M. ibid. p304.

[8] BECKWORTH, M. ibid. p279.

[9] RUGGLES, C. *Ancient Astronomy*. Santa Barbara U.S.A.: ABC-CLIO p178.

[10] LILIUOKALANI, ibid.

[11] RALOFF, J. (23/1/2009) Darkness, Melatonin May Stall Breast and Prostate Cancers: ScienceNews: http://www.sciencenews.org/view/generic/id/40170/title/Darkness,_melatonin_may_stall_breast_and_prostate_cancers_ [accessed 3/2/2009]

[12] BECKWORTH, M. Ibid. p306.

[13] MALY, K. (2001) *An Overview of The Hawaiian Cultural Landscape*. Kumupono. http://kumupono.com/Hawaiian%20Cultural%20Landscape.pdf.

CHAPTER 8
[1] LAKDAWALLA, E. (30/7/2005) *The Planetary Society Weblog*. http://www.planetary.org/blog/article/00000176/ [accessed 27/8/2006]

[2] Taken from leaflet issued with a video. Xena Warrior Princess Video© 1996 Universal Television Enterprises, Inc. as assigned to Studio USA Television Distribution LLC. Universal Pictures (UK) Ltd.

[3] TINDOL, R. (2006) *The Dwarf Planet Formerly Known As Xena Has Officially Been Named Eris, IAU Announces;* Caltech Media Relations: http://pr.caltech.edu/media/Press_Releases?PR12893.html

[4] TINDOL, R. ibid.

[5] SEYFFERT, O. (1894) *Dictionary of Classical Antiquities*. Ancient Library. http://www.ancientlibrary.com/seyffert/0228.html [accessed 2/3/2009]

[6] SEYFFERT. O. ibid.

[7] SEYFFERT, O. ibid. p225.

[8] HAYS, M. H. (1918) *Notes on the Works And Days of Hesiod*. Ph.D. Dissertation, Faculty of the Graduate School of Arts and Literature, University of Chicago. http://www.archive.org/stream/notesonworksdays00haysrich/notesonworksdays00haysrich_djvu.txt [accessed 21/2/2009]

[9] HAYS, M. H. ibid.

[10] BULFINCH, T. (1978) *Bulfinch's Mythology*. U.S.A. Avenel.

CHAPTER 9
[1] BROWN, M. (2004) *Sedna*. Caltech http://www.gps.caltech.edu/per cent7Embrown/sedna/ [accessed 27/08/2006]

[2] BROWN, M. Sedna. ibid.

[3] BROWN, M. Sedna. ibid.

[4] BROWN, M. Sedna. ibid.

[5] BOAS, F. (1888) Sedna and the Fulmar. *in* FOWKE, E. (ed) *Folklore of Canada*. Ontario, Canada: The Canadian Publishers, pp41–42.

[6] HEFNER, A. (2002-2007) Sedna. Mythical Folk. http://www.themystica.org/mythical-folk/~articles/s/sedna.html

[7] HEFNER, A. (2002-2007) *Adlivun* Mythical Folk. http://www.themystica.org/mythical-folk/~articles/a/adlivun.html

[8] KENTON, M. (2005, July 26) *The Animal and the Human*. EzineArticles. http://www.ezinearticles.com/?The-Animal-and-the-Human&id=54222 [accessed 30/8/06]

[9] ROHDE, D. (11/11/2003) *On the Common Ancestors of All Living Humans;* Massachusetts Institute of Technology: http//citeseerx.ist.psu.edu

[10] PIDWIRNY, M. (Lead Author); WALSER, M. L. (Topic Editor). 2007. "Earth's climatic history." In: Encyclopedia of Earth. Eds. Cutler J. Cleveland (Washington, D.C.: Environmental Information Coalition, National Council for Science and the Environment). [Published in the Encyclopedia of Earth December 31, 2007; Retrieved May 9, 2009]. http://www.eoearth.org/article/Earth's_climatic_history

[11] POBOJEWSKI, S. (Oct 26 1992) *Changes in lakes levels 10,000 years ago could explain global chill*. News and Information Services. http://www.umich.edu/~urecod/9293/Oct26_92/22.htm [accessed 4/9/2006]

[12] National Academy of Sciences. (2006) *Abrupt Climate Change: Inevitable Surprises*. National Academy of Sciences. http://dels.nas.edu/abr_clim/evidence.shtml [accessed 2/9/2006]

[13] ANON (29/7/2003) *Abrupt Climate Change;* National Geophysical Data Center. http://www.ngdc.noaa.gov/paleo/ctl/abrupt.html [accessed 4/9/2006]

[14] MOULTON HOWE, L. (2002) *What Happened That Killed So Many Animals?* Cambodia News online. http://www.cambodianonline.net/earth02002.htm [accessed 27/8/2006]

[15] SCHWARTZ, J. (24/10/2001) *Blame North American Megafauna Extinction on Climate Change, Not Human Ancestors*. University of Washington. http://www.washington.edu/newsroom/news/2001archive/10-01archive/k102401.html [accessed 10/5/2009]

[16] TOWNSEND, M., and HARRIS, P. (Feb 22nd 2004) *Now the Pentagon tells Bush: climate change will destroy us*. Guardian Unlimited http;//www.guardian.co.uk/usa/story/0,12271,1153531,00.html [accessed 31/8/2006]

[17] U. S. Environmental Protection Agency. (2006) *Global Warming News and Events, Science and Policy News*. U.S. Environmental Protection Agency. http:Yosemite.epa.gov/oar/global warming.nsf/content/News and eventsScience and Policy News.html [accessed 31/8/2006]

[18] McCARTHY, M. and USBORNE, D. (15/9/2006) *Massive Surge In Disappearance of Arctic Sea Ice Sparks Global Warming*. The Independent. No 6212. pp1–5.

[19] ANON. (March 2007) *About IPY: International Polar Year:* http://www.ipy.org/index.php?/ipy/about/ [accessed 3rd May 2009]

[20] ANON. (9/5/2009) *Polar Bear Week With Nigel Marvin*. Channel Five Broadcasting Corporation. [watched 9/5/2009]

[21] RICHARD-VAN MAELE, C. (7/8/2007) The World Meteorological Organization Reports on Extreme Weather and Climate Events. World Meteorological Office. http://www.wmo.int/pages/mediacentre/press_releasespr_791_en.html [accessed 3/5/2009]

[22] ANON. (2008) *2004: Thousands Die in Asian Tsunami*. BBC. http://news.bbc.co.uk/onthisday/hi/dates/stories/december/26/newsid_4631000/4631713.stm [accessed 5/5/2008]

[23] ANON. (15/8/2005) Tsunami Clue to Atlantis Found BBC News. http://news.bbc.co.uk/1/hi/sci/tech/4153008.stm [accessed 31/8/2006]

[24] ORNELAS, G. Atlantis Rises Again. *Science Magazine*; http://sciencenow.sciencemag.org/cgi/content/full/2005/722/1 [accessed 10/5/2009]

[25] ANON. (2006) Science and Policy News. U.S. Environmental Protection Agency. http://yosemite.epa.gov/oar/globalwarming.nsf/content/NewsandeventsScienceandPolicynews.html [accessed 31/8/2006]

[26] BROWN, R. (May 2005) *Sedna Astrological Meaning: evolving thoughts*. Karma Astrology. http://www.karmastrology.com/Sedna-meaning.shtml [accessed 27/08/2006]

[27] ANON. (19/8/1998) *Rise In fires Began 10,000 Years Ago*. Forests.Org: http://forests.org/archive/general/risefire.htm [accessed 27/8/2006]

[28] ANON, 1/5/2010 Record Breaking Current Found Deep in Southern Ocean. *New Scientist*. http://www.newscientist.com/article/mg20627583.100-recordbreaking-current-found-deep-in-southern-ocean.html [accessed on 26/5/2010]

[29] LOVETT, A. (14/4/2010) Ebbing sunspot activity makes Europe freeze. *Naturenews*. http://www.nature.com/news/2010/100414/full/news.2010.184.html [accessed 26/5/2010]

[30] BROWN, R. (May 2005) *Sedna Astrological Meaning Evolving Thoughts*. Karma Astrology. http://www.karmastrology.com/Sedna-meaning.shtml [accessed 27/08/2006]

[31] ANON. (March 2007) *About IPY*; International Polar Year: http://www.ipy.org/index.php?/ipy/about/ [accessed May 3rd 2009]

CHAPTER 10
[1] HAYS, M. H. (1918) Notes on the Works and Days of Hesiod. PH. D. Dissertaion, Faculty of the graduate School of Arts and Leterature, University of Chicago. http://wwwarchive.org/stream/notesonworksdays00haysrich_djvu.txt [accessed 21/2/2009]

[2] MILTON, J. (1667) Paradise Lost: New Arts Library: http://www.paradiselost.org/novel.html [accessed 3/3/2009]

[3] BLAVATSKY, H. (1888) The Secret Doctrine: sacredtexts.com: http://www.sacred-texts.com/the/sd/index.htm

[4] MEAD, G. R. S. (1906) Thrice Great Hermes Vol 2: Sacred Texts: http://www.sacred-texts.com/gno/th2/index.htm

CHAPTER 11
[1] ANON. Native Americans/ Migration Stories/ The Genographic Project; https://genographic.nationalgeographic.com/genographic/lan/en/globe.html#/ms046/

[2] STRAY, G. (2007) *The Mayan and Other Ancient Calendars*. Glastonbury; Wooden Books Ltd

[3] BARNHART, Dr. E. The Long Count and 2012 AD. Maya Exploration Centre. http://www.mayan-calendar.com/ancient_longcount.html

[4] BARNHART, Dr. E. ibid

[5] STRAY, G. (2007) *The Mayan and Other Ancient Calendars*. Glastonbury; Wooden Books Ltd.

[6] STRAY, G. (2007) ibid.

[7] FAGAN, B. (2001) *The Seventy Great Mysteries of the Ancient World*. London: Thames and Hudson Ltd.

[8] BROWN, M. (7/6/2009) *Sony Pictures And The End Of The World*. Mike Brown's Planets; http://www.mikebrownsplanets.com/

[9] TOWNSEND, J and DUNBAR, B. (9/11/09) *2012. Beginning of the End or Why the World Won't End?* NASA; http://www.nasa.gov/topics/earth/features/2012.html

[10] KRUPP, E.C. *The Great 2012 Doomsday Scare*. NASA; http://www.nasa.gov/topics/earth/features/2012-guest.html [accessed 17/12/2009]

[11] MAJOR JENKINS, J. *What Is the Galactic Alignment?* Alignment 2012; http://www.alignment2012.com/whatisGA.htm [accessed 17/12/2009]

[12] WATZKE, M. et al (24/4/2006) *Nasa's Chandra Finds Black Holes Are Green.* Chandra X-ray observatory http://chandra.harvard.edu/press/06_releases/press_042406.html

[13] ROBBINS, S. (4/2/2009) *Planet X and 2012: What The Sky Looks Like On December 21, 2012;* Exposing PseudoAstronomy; http://pseudoastro.wordpress.com/2009/02/04/planet-x-and-2012-what-the-sky-looks-like-on-december-21-2012/

[14] KRUPP, E.C. *The Great 2012 Doomsday Scare.* NASA; http://www.nasa.gov/topics/earth/features/2012-guest.html [accessed 17/12/2009]

[15] MACKENZIE, D. (1915) *Myths of Babylonia and Assyria.* Sacred Texts. http://www.sacred-texts.com/ane/mba/index.htm

[16] KING, L. (1902) *The Seven Tablets of Creation.* Sacred Texts. http://www.sacred-texts.com/ane/stc/stc10.htm

[17] PRITCHARD, J. (1955) *Ancient Near East Texts Relating to the Old Testament.* Princeton, New Jersey. Princeton University Press.

[18] BOURNE, J. (2006) *The Vaulting Pole.* National Geographic. Vol 210/6

[19] DENLINGER, M. *Auroras, Paintings in the Sky.* Regents of the University of California; http://www.exploratorium.edu/learning_studio/auroras/happen.html

[20] NAVE, R. (2005) *The Dynamo Effect, Earth's Magnetic Field.* Hyperphysics at Georgia State University. http://hyperphysics.phy-astr.gsu.edu/hbasees/magnetic/MagEarth.html [accessed 13/12/2009]

[21] BERGERON, L. (30/3/1996) When North Flies South. Birds Could Loose Their Bearings and Geophysicists Their Precious Theories When.. *New Scientist.* http://www.newscientist.com/article/mg14920234.100-when-north-flies-south--birds-could-lose-their-bearings-and-geophysicists-their-precious-theories-when-the-earths-magnetic-field-flips-lou-bergeron-asks-just-how-fast-it-could-happen.html?full=true

[22] BRAHIC, C. (30/4/2008) Birds Can 'See' the Earth's Magnetic Field: *New Scientist.* http://www.newscientist.com/article/dn13811-birds-can-see-the-earths-magnetic-field.html [accessed 13/12/2009]

[23] TAYLOR, K. (31/10/2009) Birds Navigate by Seeing Magnetic Field Lines. *New Scientist,* 204(2732) p18.

[24] ESPENAK, F (13/7/2005) 2004 and 2012 Transits of Venus. NASA; http://eclipse.gsfc.nasa.gov/transit/venus0412.html

[25] CHAPMAN, D. (23/3/2009) Venus Moves From the Evening Star to the Morning Star. 365 Days of Astronomy. http://365daysofastronomy.org/2009/03/23/march-23rd/

[26] HERGENROTHER, C. (9/3/2009) Venus Approaching Inferior Conjunction. The Transient Sky, Comets, Asteroids, Meteors. http://transientsky.wordpress.com/2009/03/09/venus/

[27] IWANISZEWSKI, S. (2005) Venus in the East and West. in Chamberlain et al, (ed) Songs From the Sky, Indigenous Astronomical and Cosmological Traditions of the World. PO21 5HD Ocarina Books. pp151–162.

[28] BLITZER, C. (1969) *Age of Kings.* Netherlands. Time Inc.

[29] BLITZER, C. (1969) ibid

[30] ANON, (5/8/2008) *Time Line, Northern Rock Bank Crisis.* BBC News. http://news.bbc.co.uk/1/hi/business/7007076.stm [accessed 15/12/2009]

[31] The words of one Indigo I know well, my daughter, Jessica.

[32] ABHEDANANDA, S. (1902) *How to be a Yogi* Sacred Texts: http://www.sacred-texts.com/hin/hby/hby03.htm

[33] GREENE, L. (1983) *The Outer Planets and the Collective:* CRCS Publications; California, U.S.A. pp 172.

[34] GREENE, L ibid p168.

ILLUSTRATIONS

Illustrations 1–10, 12–20, 22 are by Robbi Lambert 2009© and can only be reproduced with the consent of the artist and payment of a copyright fee.

p13 **1** Pre 17th century Solar System. Designed by the author.

p14 **2** 19th century Solar System. Designed by the author.

p15 **3** 21st century Solar System.

p29 **4** Ceres. Designed by the author.

p44 **5** The Greek Underworld. Copied from Athenian Black Figure Vases by John Boardman. He describes it as a neck amphora by the Bucci painter. Souls pour water and Sisyphos rolls his stone in Hades.

p47 **6** Pluto, Proserpine, Mercury and a mortal. Copied and adapted from *The Encyclopaedia of Mythology (1996)* by Authur Cotterall, which reports it to have been copied from an earlier illustration in Dr. Smith's Classical Dictionary, 1895.

p77 **7** Charon, Hermes and a mortal. Copied from an image on www.thcoldreligion.com, source not supplied.

p86 **8** Mekemeke, the Great Sea Spirit. Copied from a drawing in William Thompson's report. This rare image was drawn by Thompson from a rock carving. The report can be seen on www.sacred-texts.com

p89 **9** Adapted from *Island At The End of The World* by S. Fischer.

p99 **10** Copy of a drawing done by a member of captain Cook's party in 1774.

p105 **11** Photocopy from *The Easter Island Tablets: Decipherments,* by A Carroll, published in the Journal of the Polynesian Society, Vol 1 (1892) This is all on the rongorongo web site at www.rongorongo.org/carroll/tahua.html

p109 **12, 13,** p111 **14** Drawn from the many different images available in books in the Reference section.

p118 **15** Drawn from an illustration by William Thompson in his report entitled *Te Pito Te Henua Or Easter Island.* www.sacred-texts.com/pac/ei/index.htm

p119 **16** Drawn from the many different images available in books in the Reference section.

p133 **17** Hawaii.

p144 **18** Eris.

p153 **19** Sedna.

p186 **20** A copy of the title page of the Fejervary screenfold.

p193 **21** Galactic Alignment drawn by the author.

p197 **22** Earth's Magnetic Poles.

Acknowledgements

My journey into astrology could not have begun without my teachers. Thanks to the knowledge of Linda Goodman, Jonathan Cainer, Melanie Reinhart, Sue Thompkins, Liz Greene, Clare Martin and Alexander Von Schlieffen amongst others.

My journey into teaching could not have begun without the request and support of Sue Orchard, manager of the Cottage Healing Centre in Tamworth, who booked me to run my first course. Thanks to Sue and all the students on that first course.

My journey into the Dwarf Planets could not have happened without the team of astronomers that discovered them, Mike Brown, Chad Trujillo and David Rabinowitz. I would like to thank them for their careful and sensitive choice of names, which made the meanings so accessible. Also thanks to astronomer Bill Law of the Walsall Astronomy Group, who supplies me with loads of astronomical stuff and believes, like I do, that astronomers and astrologers can both co-exist.

My journey could not continue without the clients who fund me and the students in my school, the Midlands School of Astrology, who support me and exchange with me. Thanks also to BBC producer Michaela Atkins and presenter Richard Spurr at BBC Radio Nottingham for my first weekly broadcasting opportunity.

Finally, thanks to my ex-husband for all the illustrations. We leave the results to our beautiful and talented daughter, Jessica, a triple Leo who surpasses us both with her courage, determination and personal achievements.

Alison Chester-Lambert, 2010